THIS BOOK BELONGS TO:

_ _ _ _ _ _ _ _ _ _ _ _ _

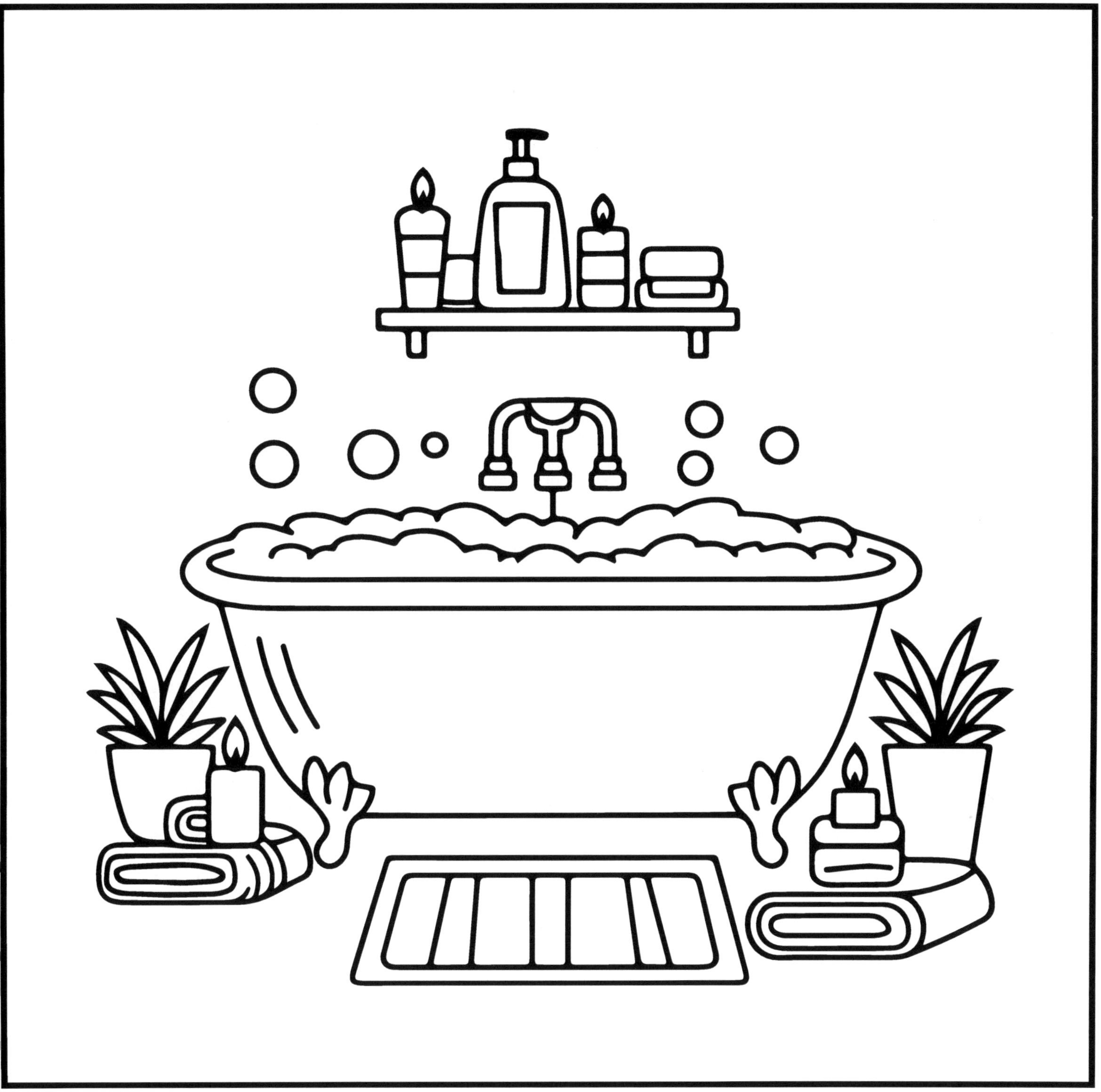

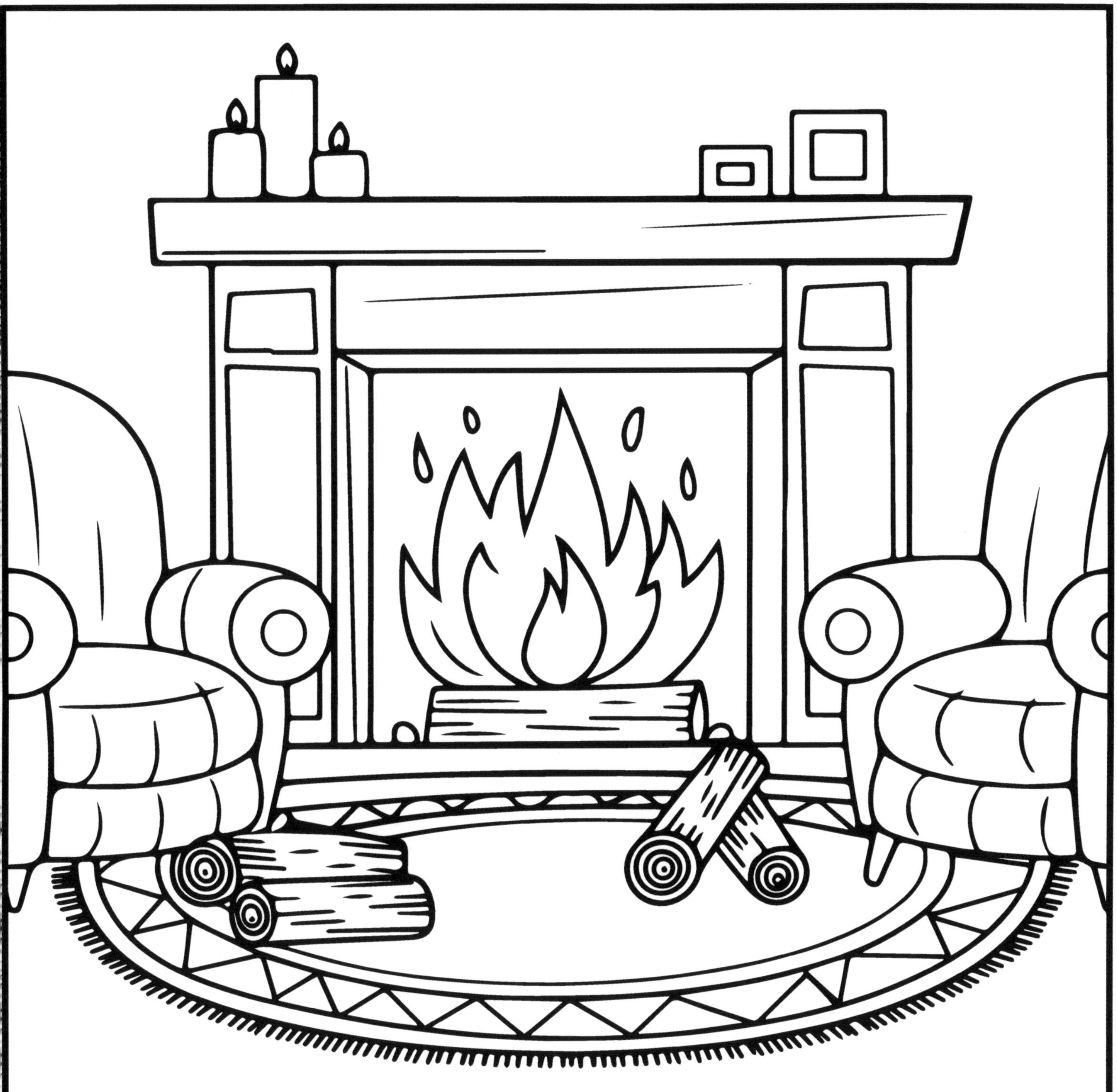

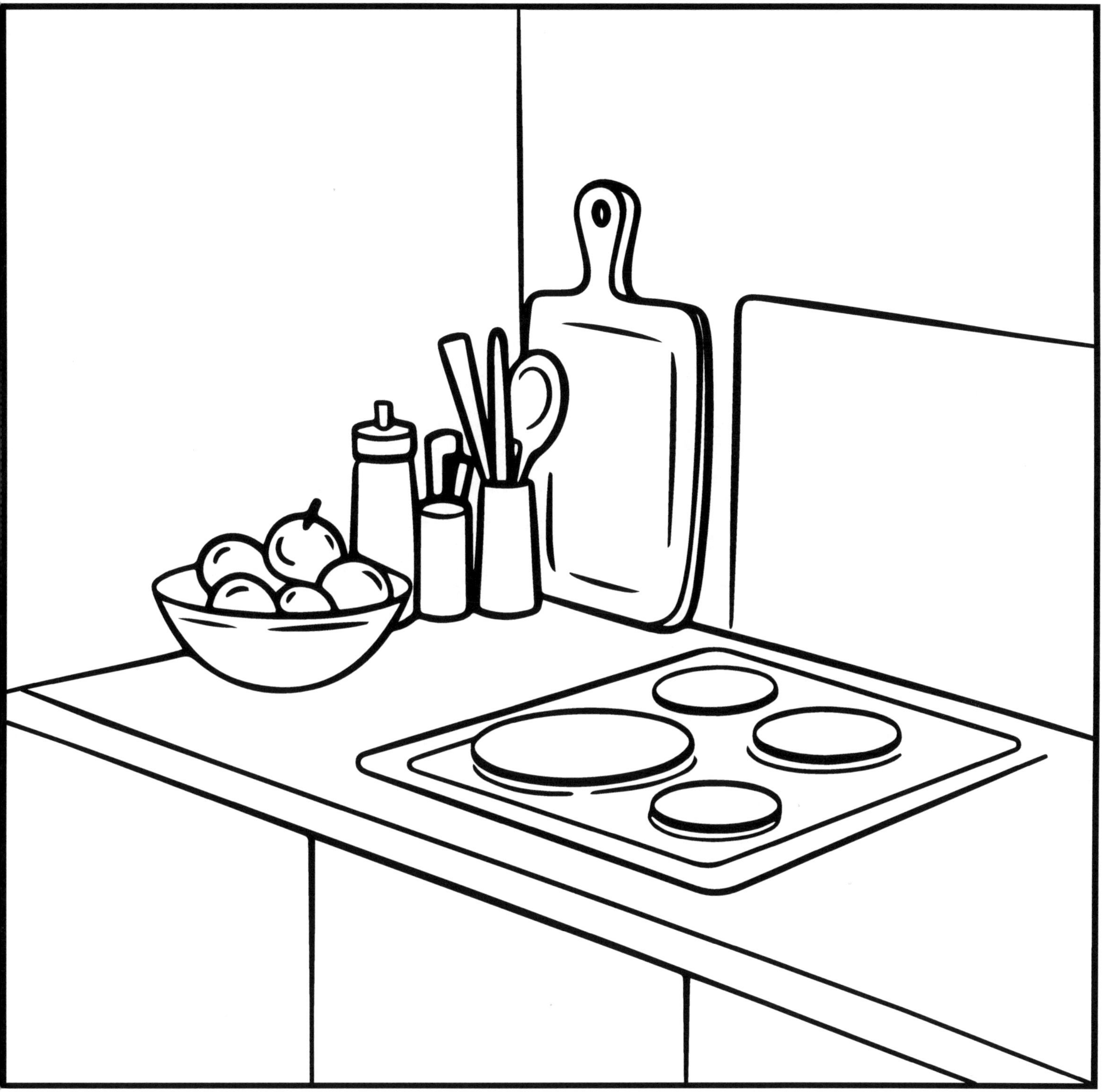

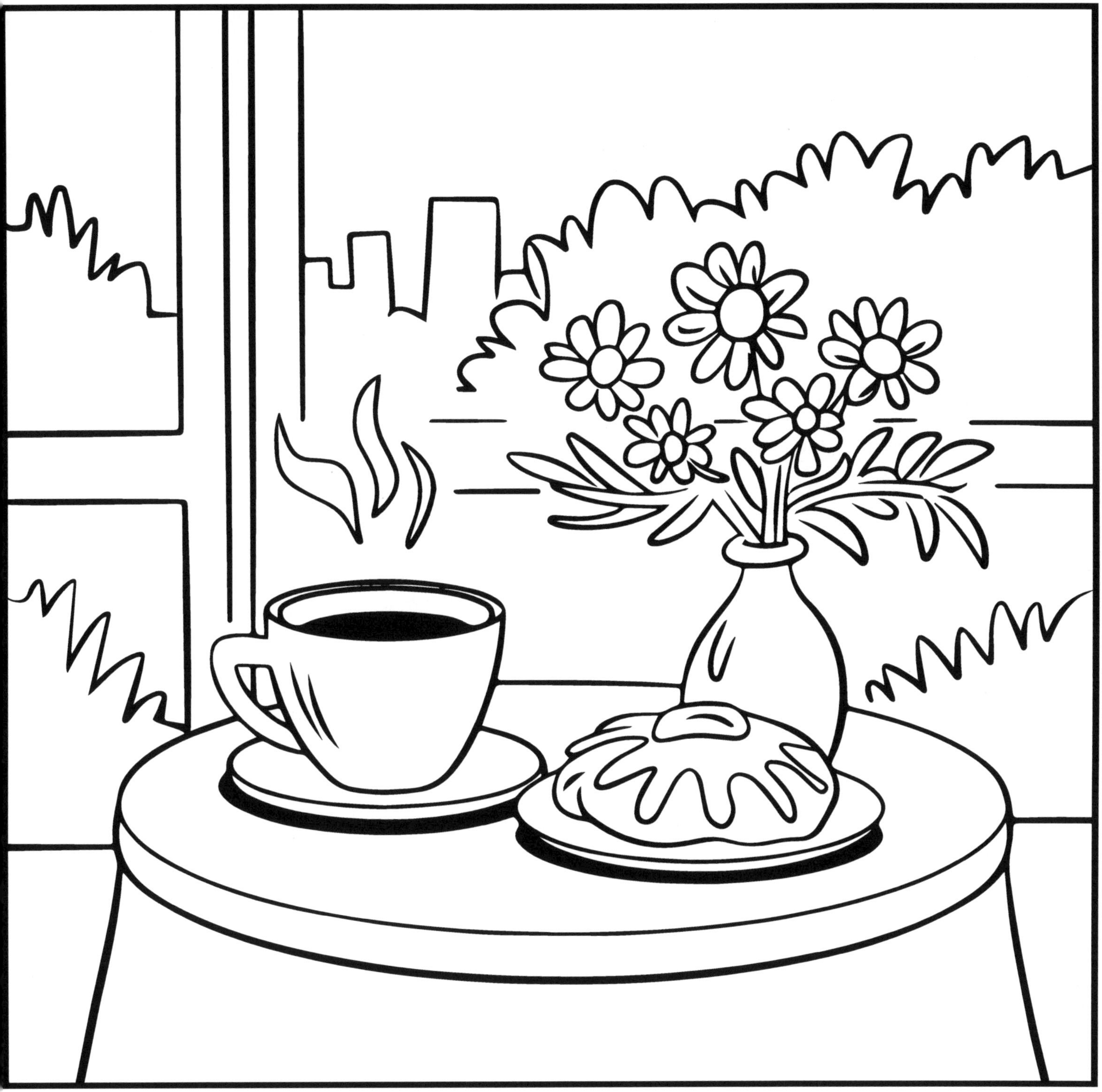

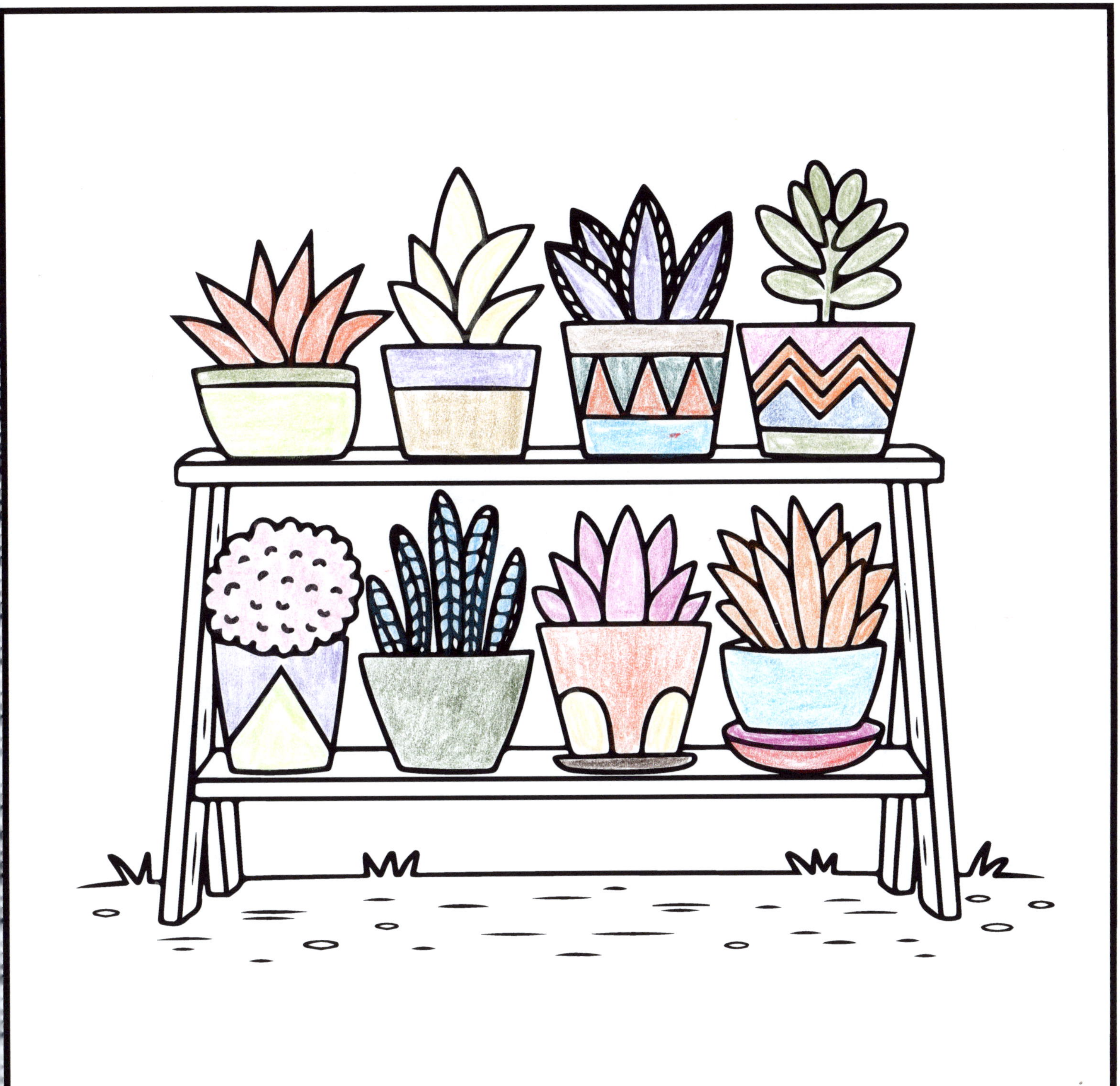

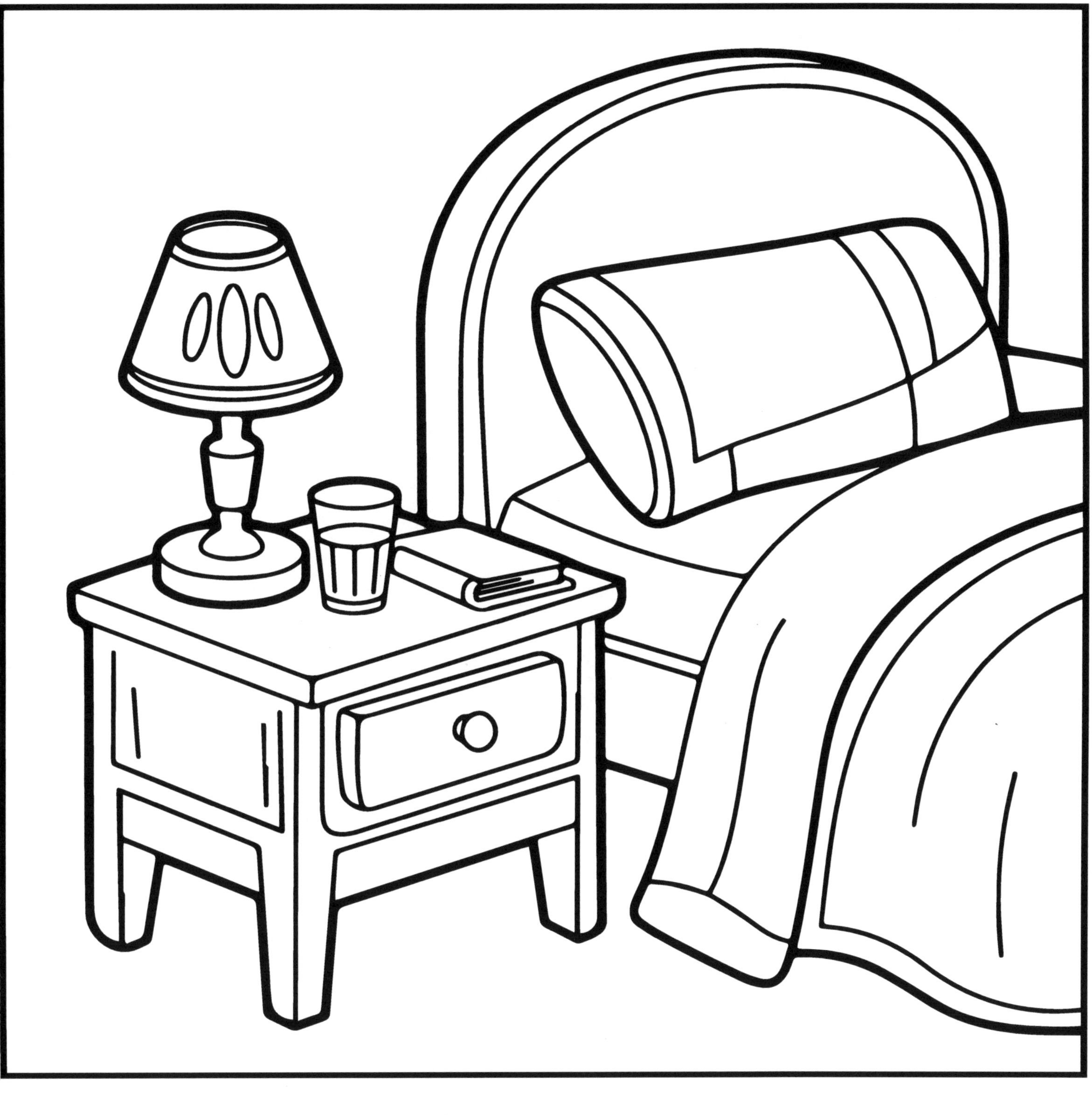

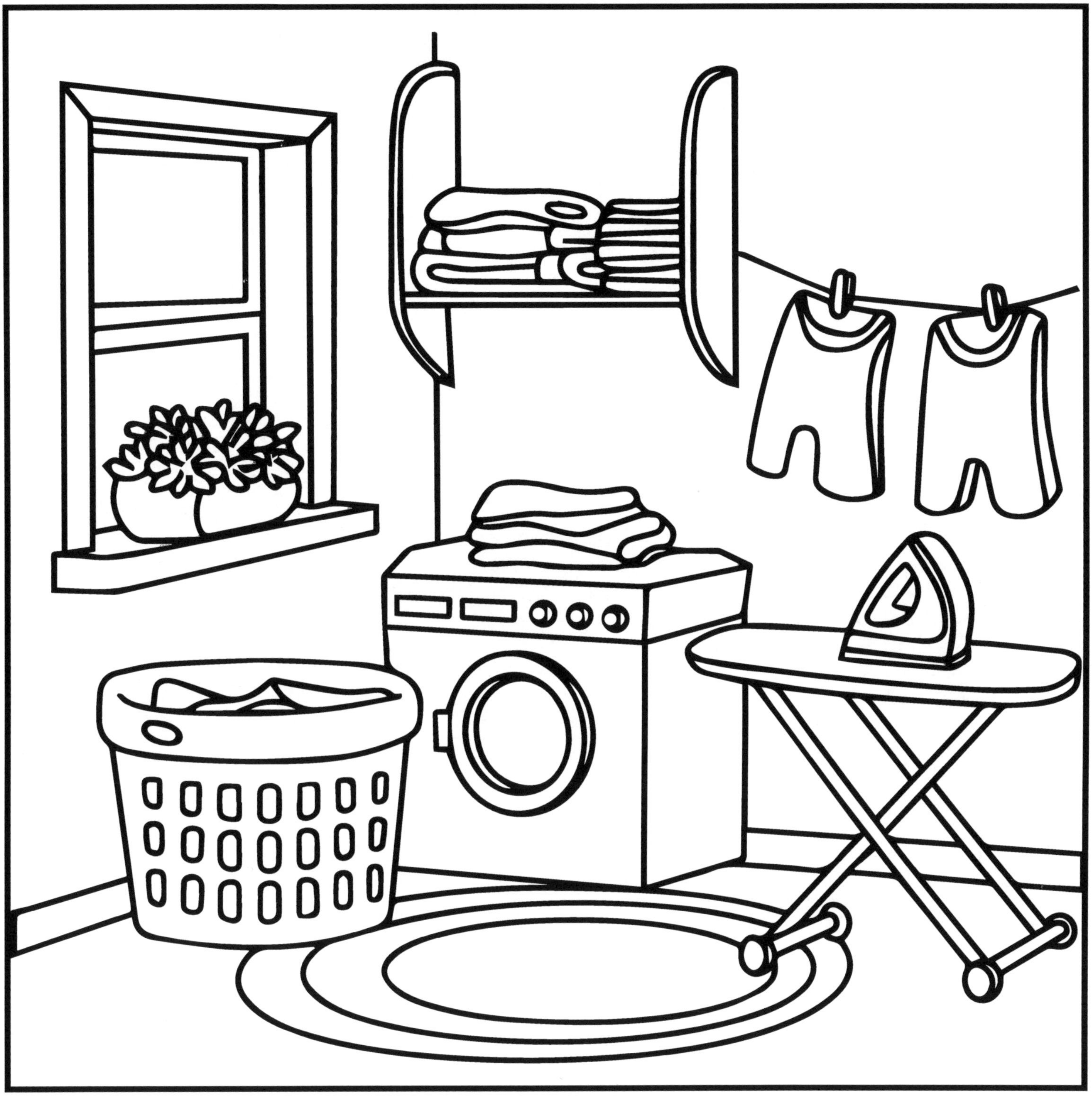

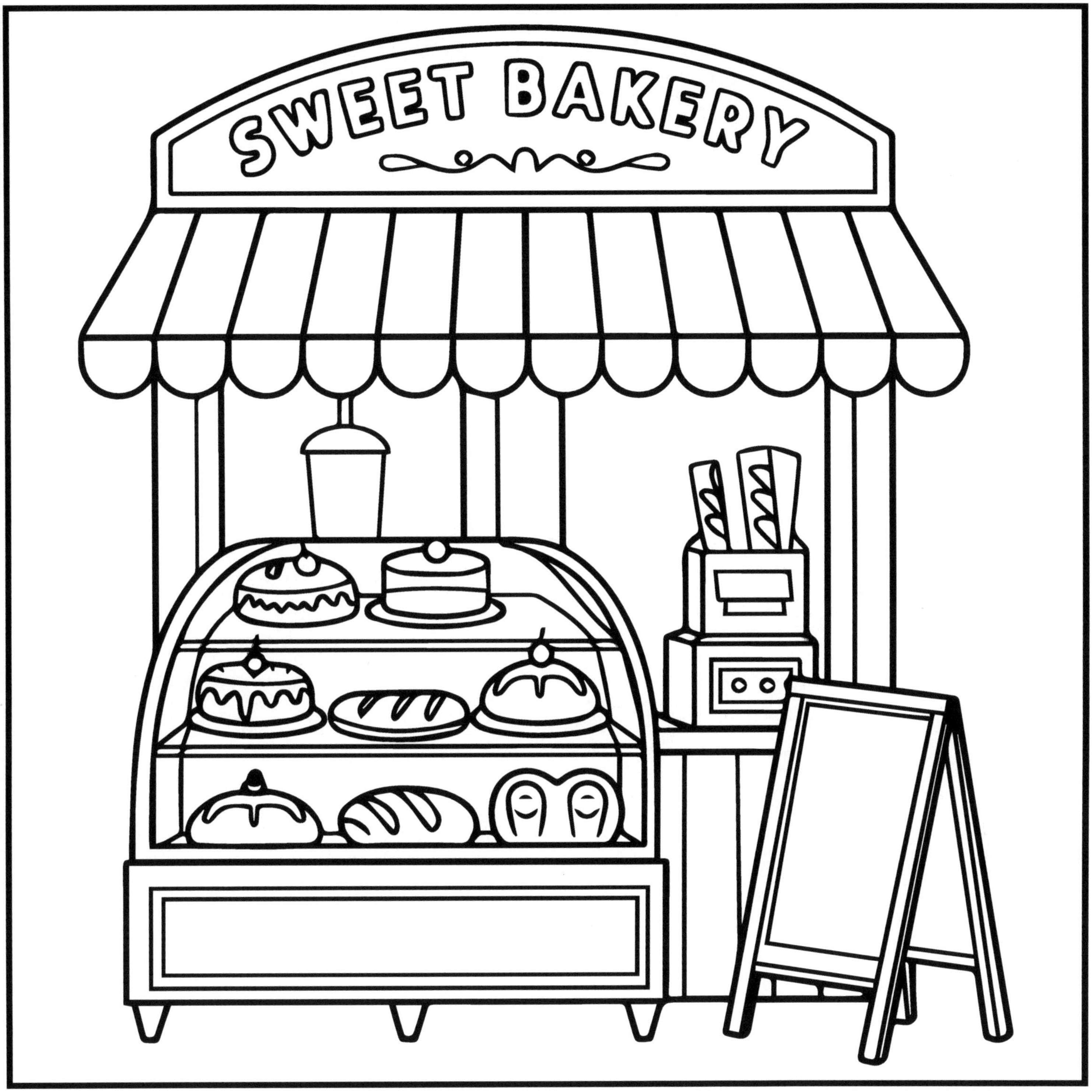
SWEET BAKERY

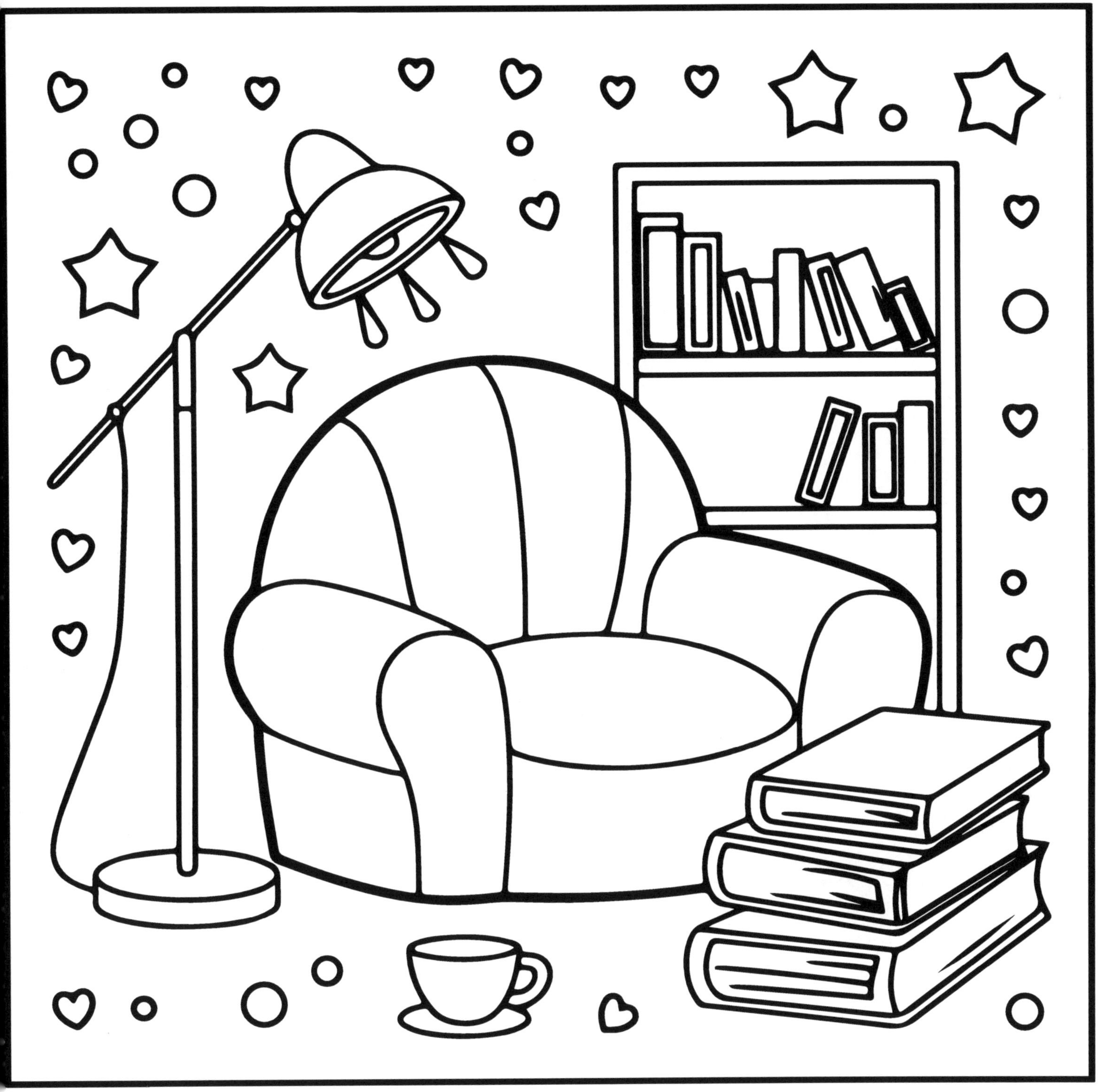

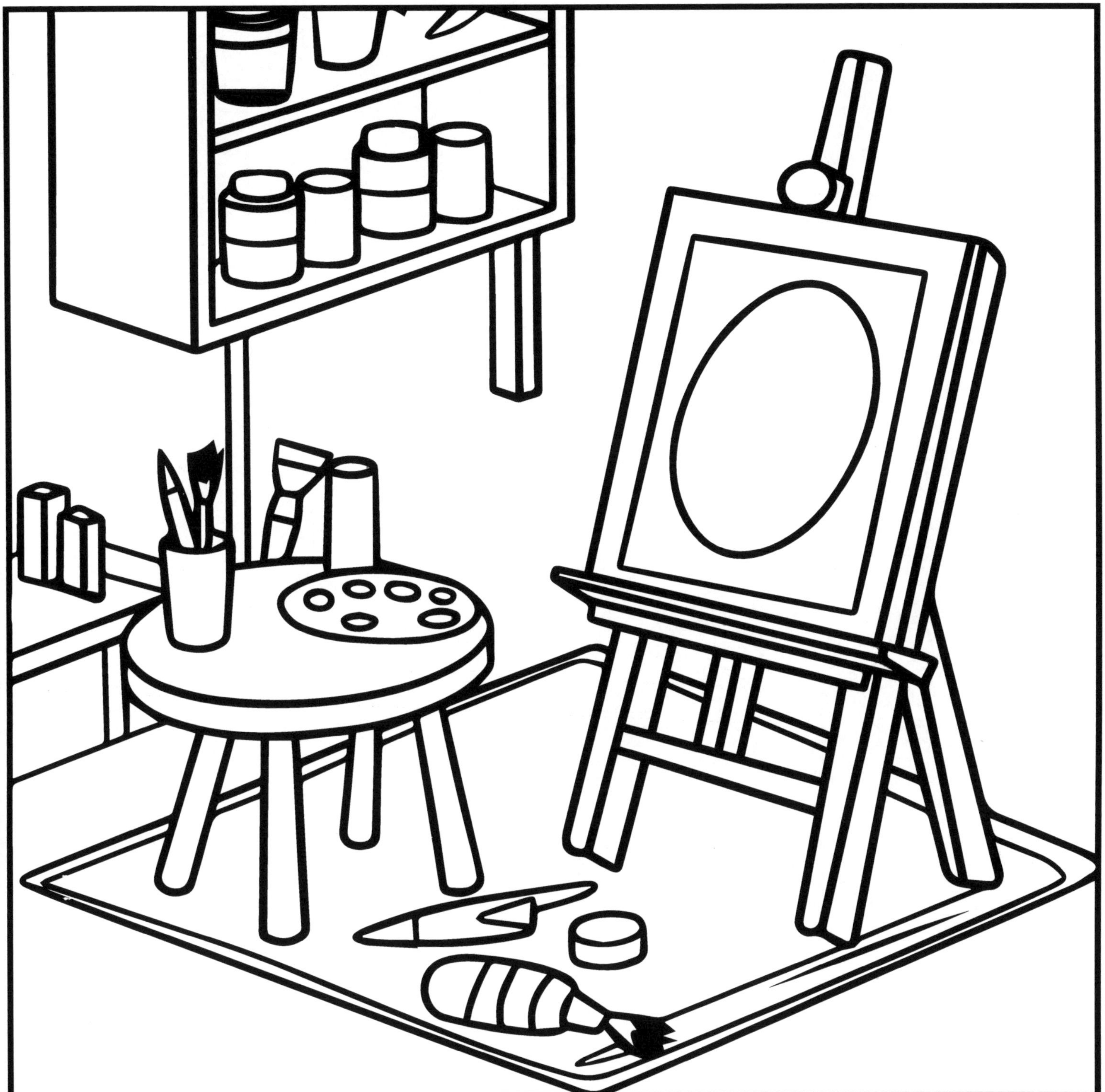

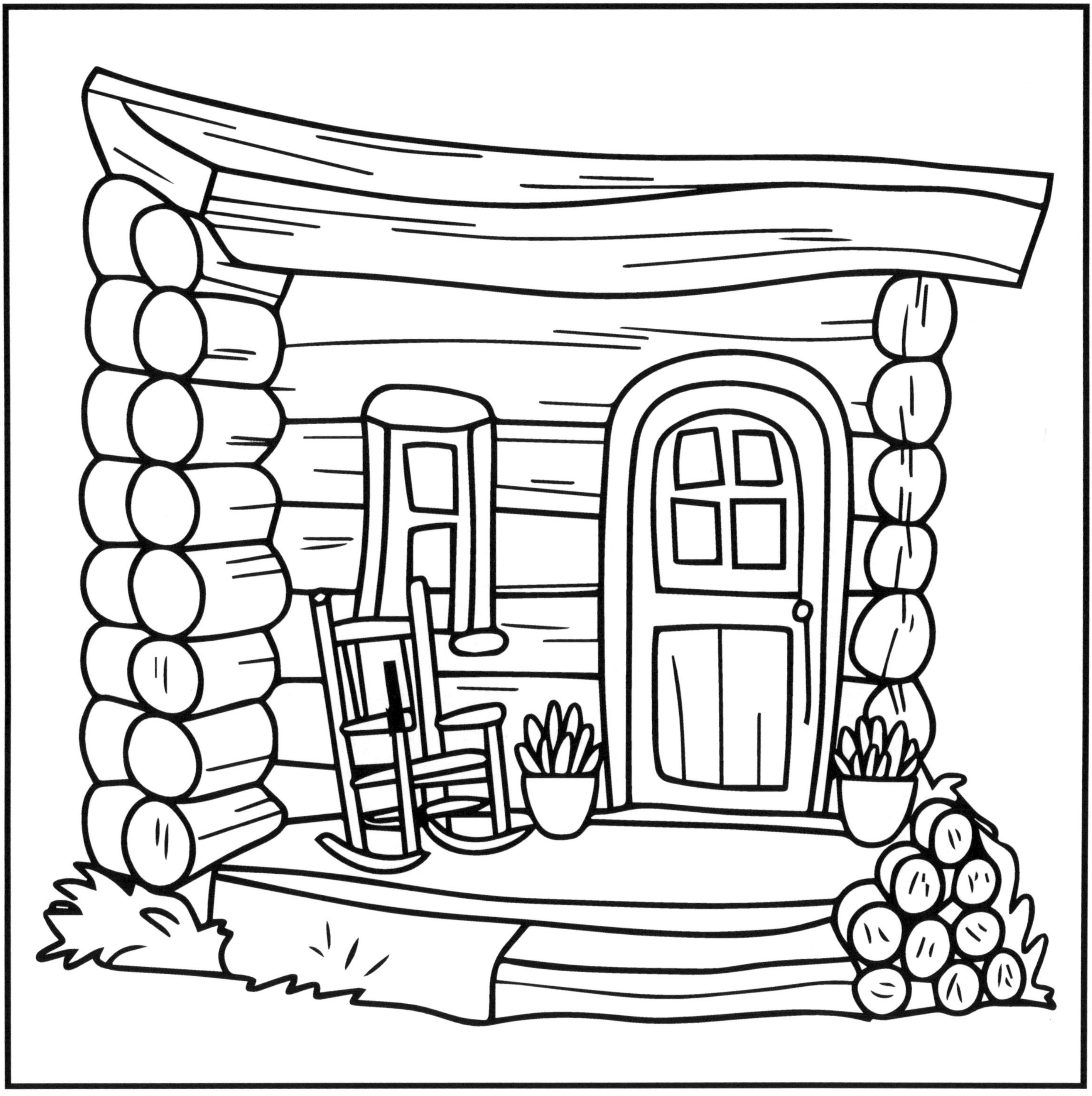

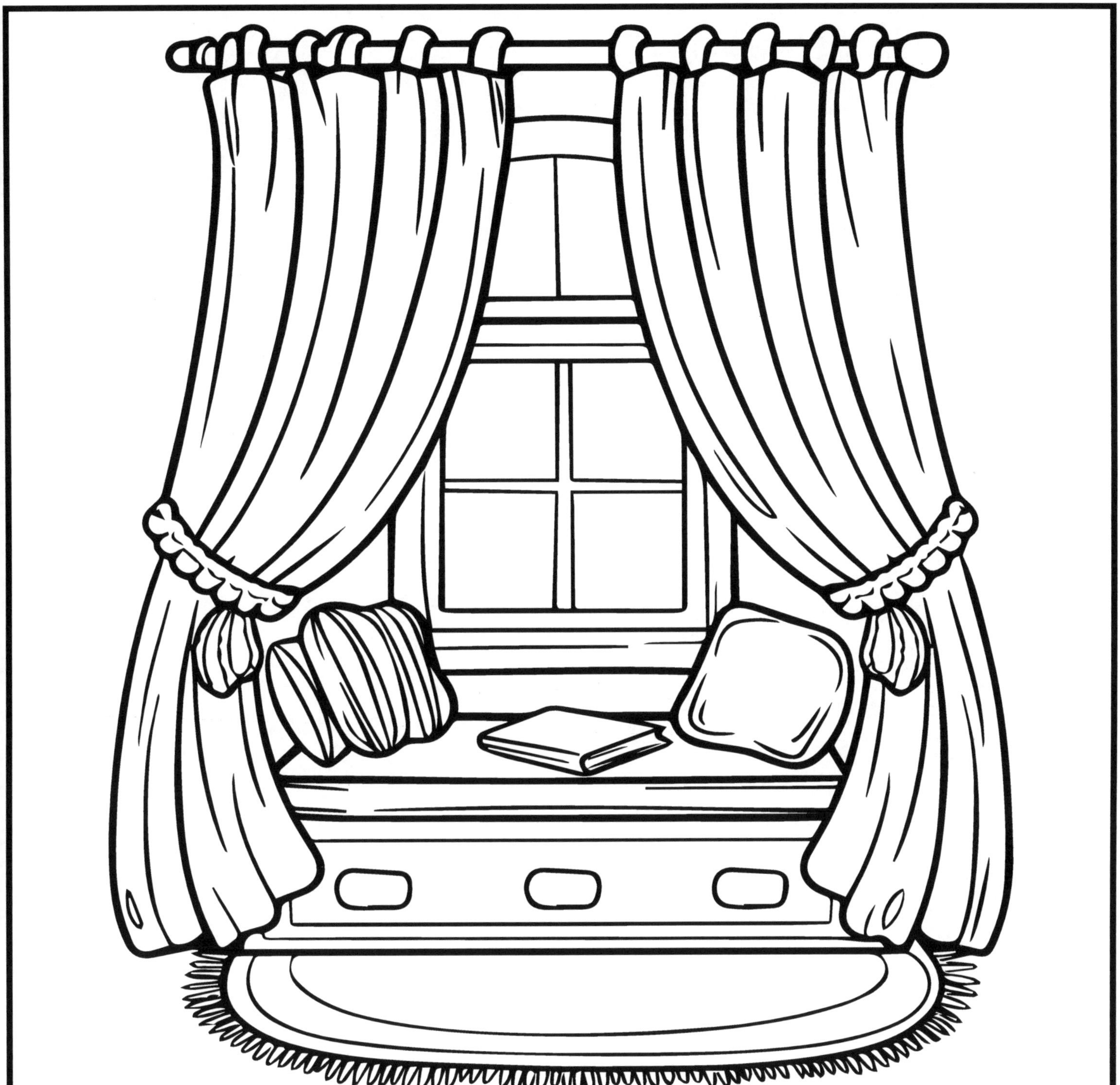

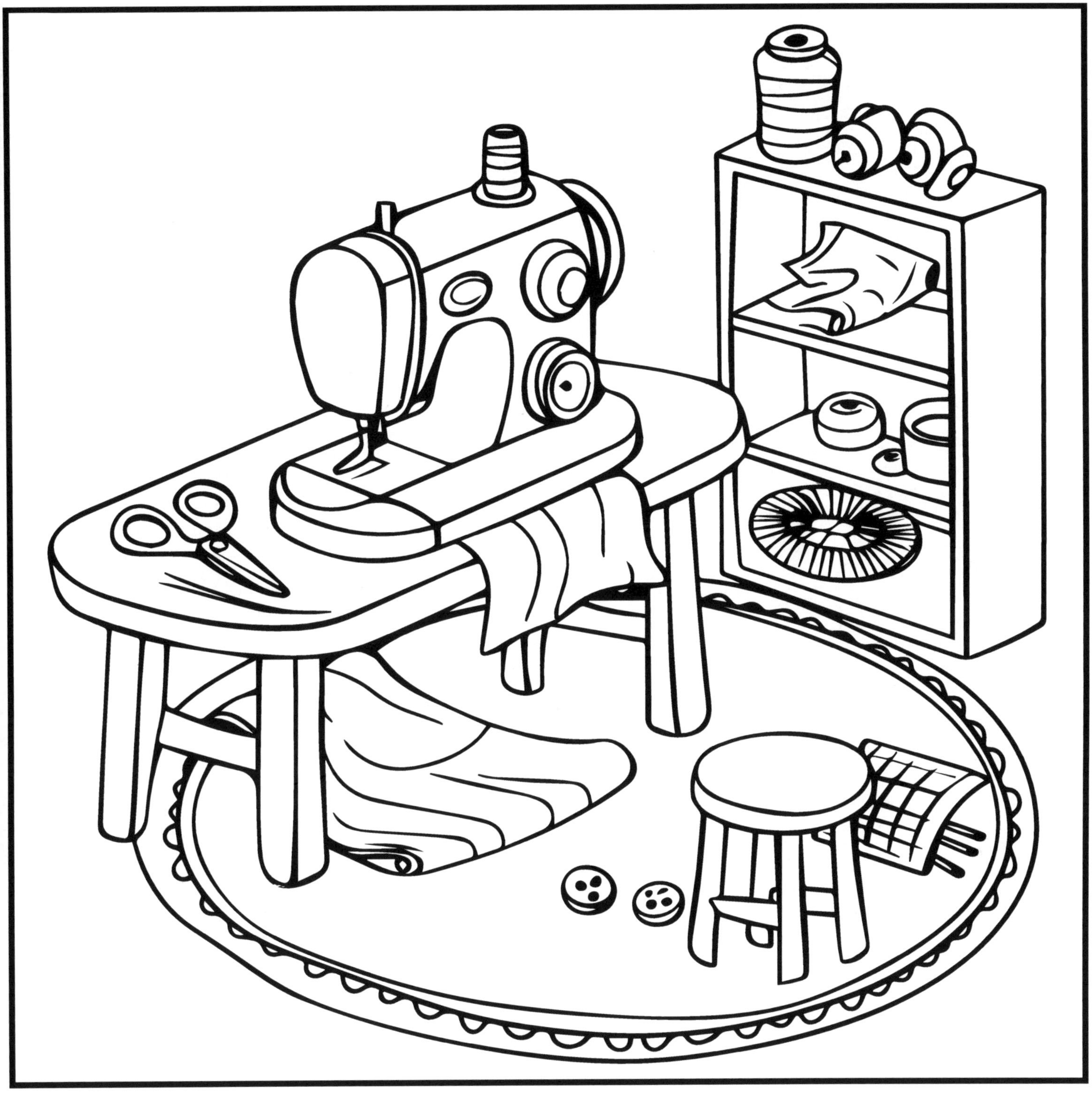

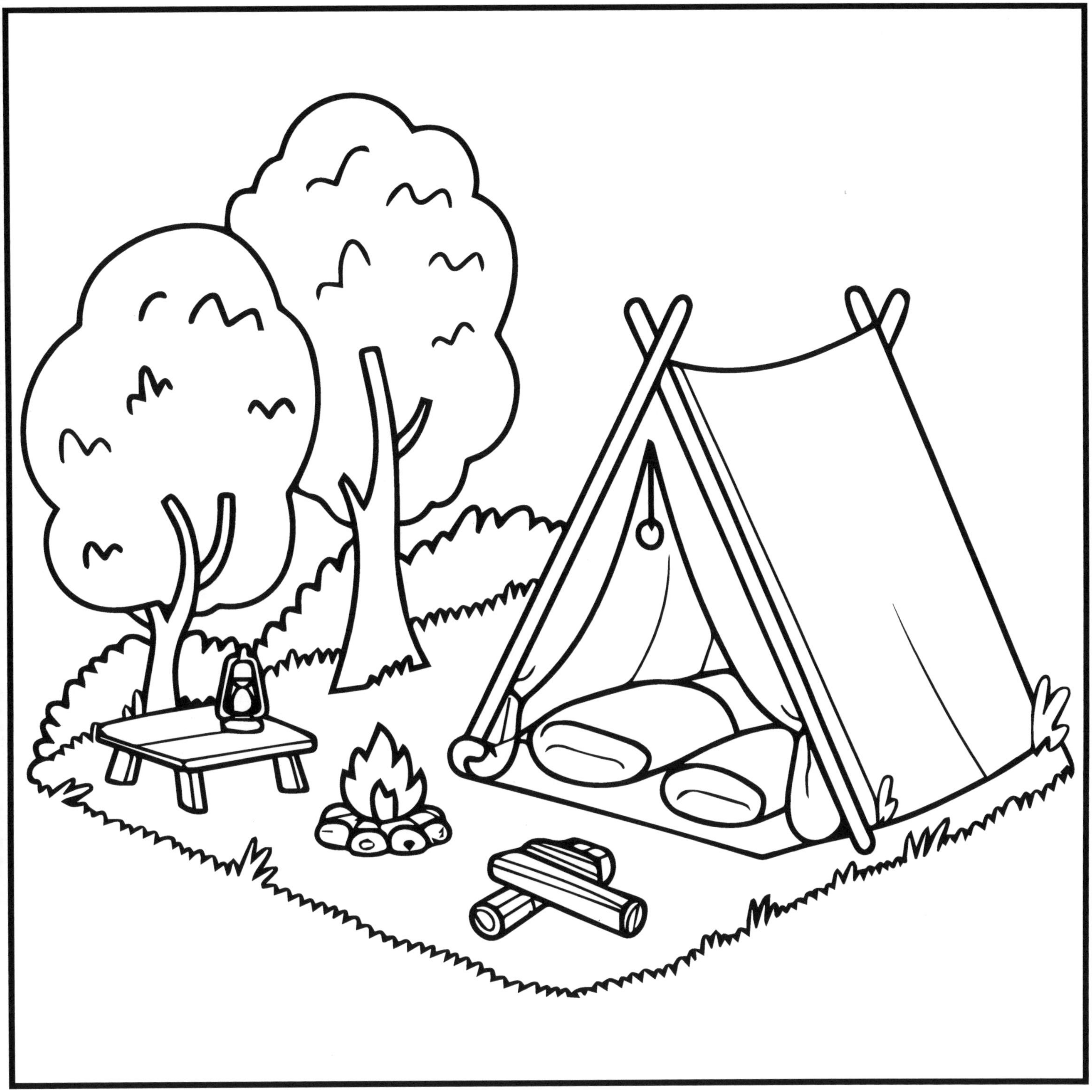

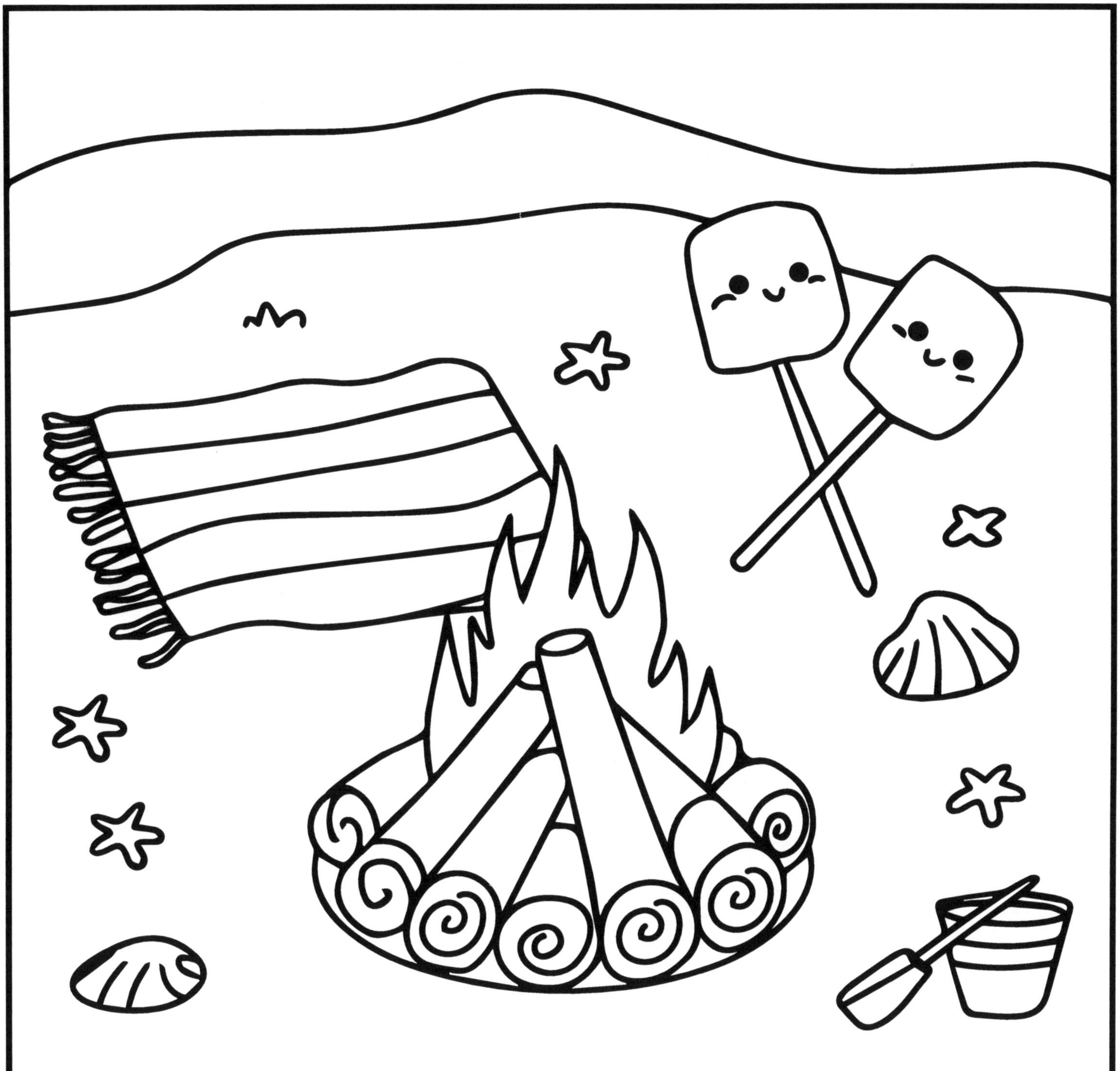

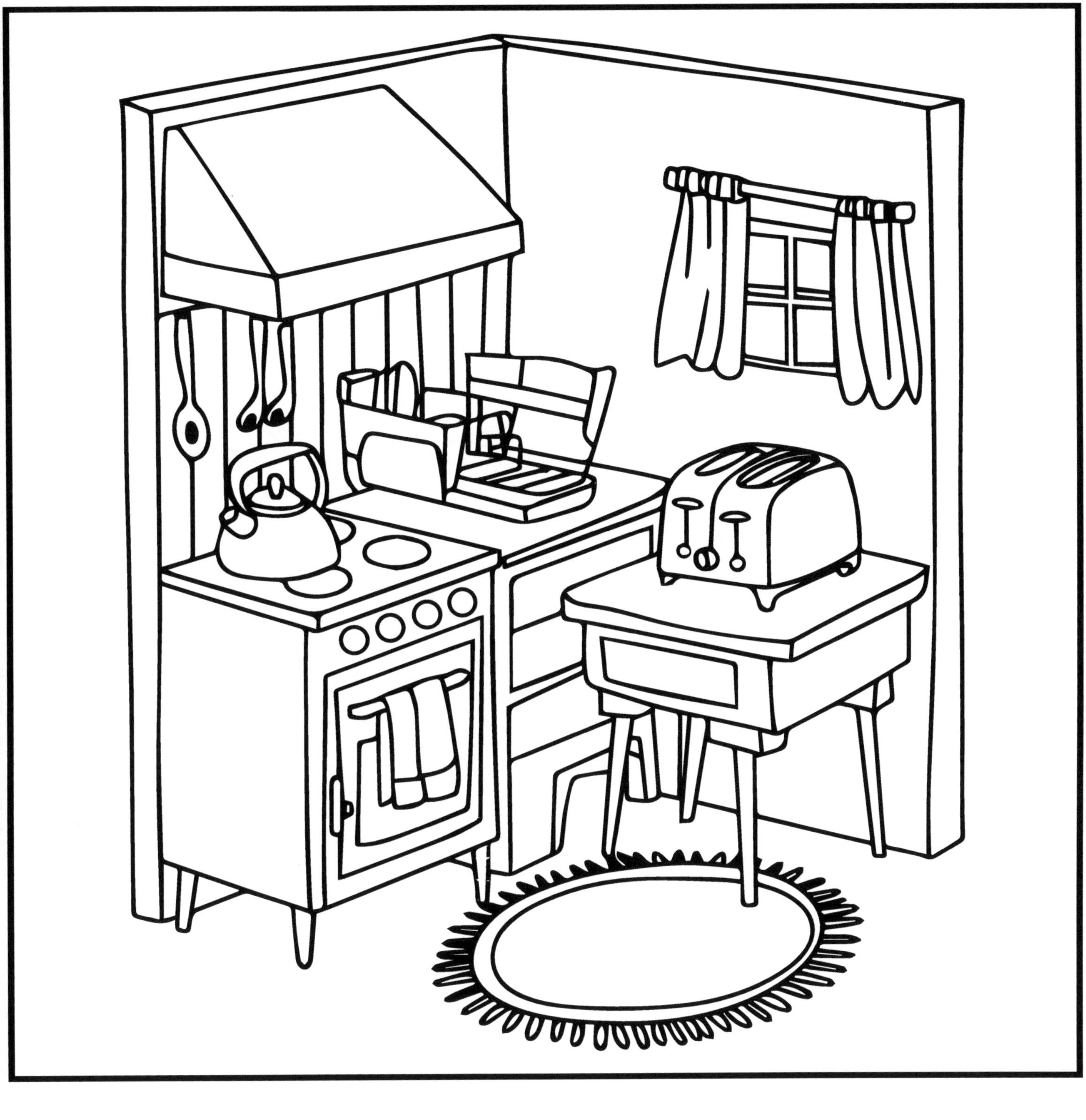

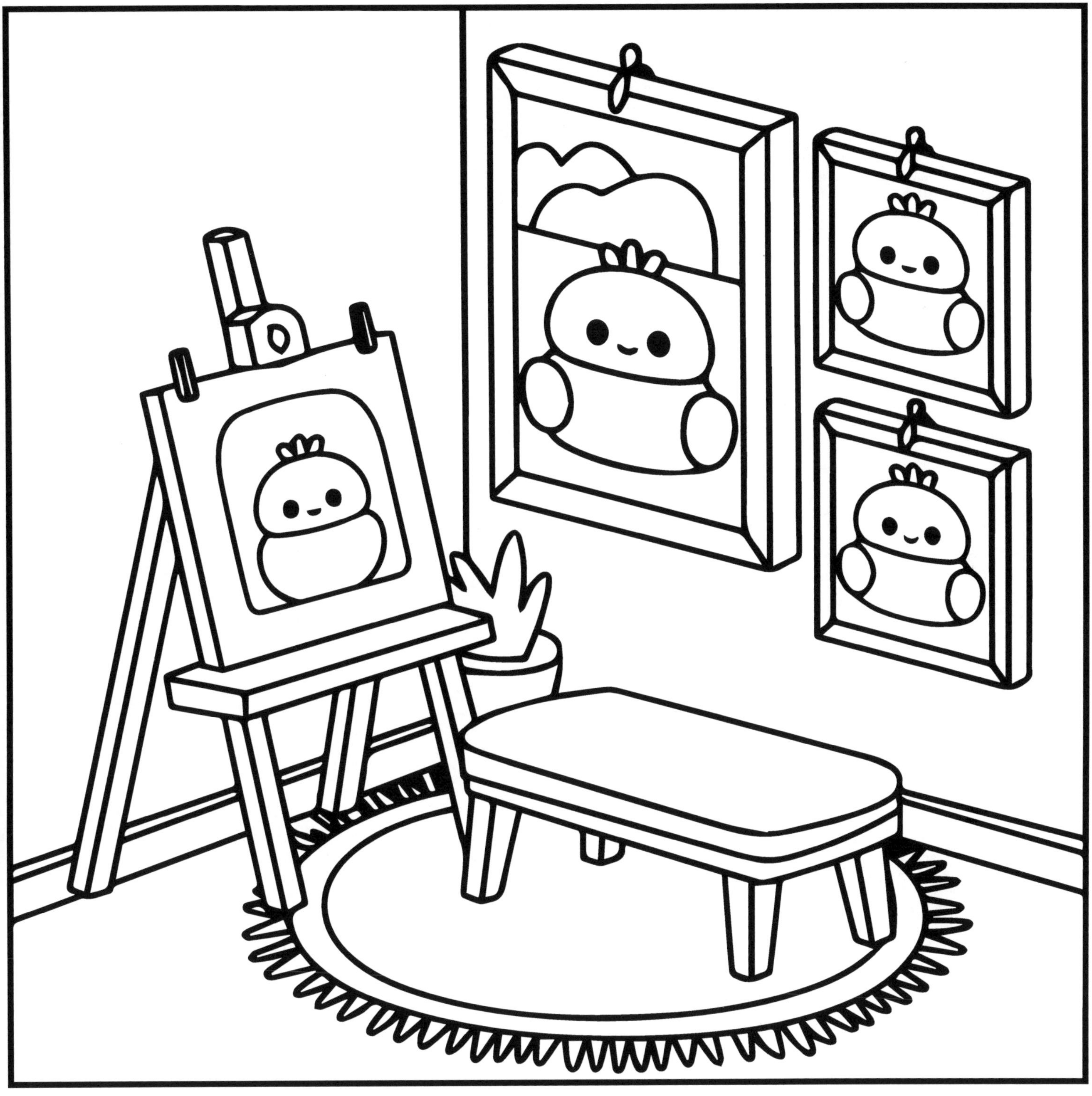

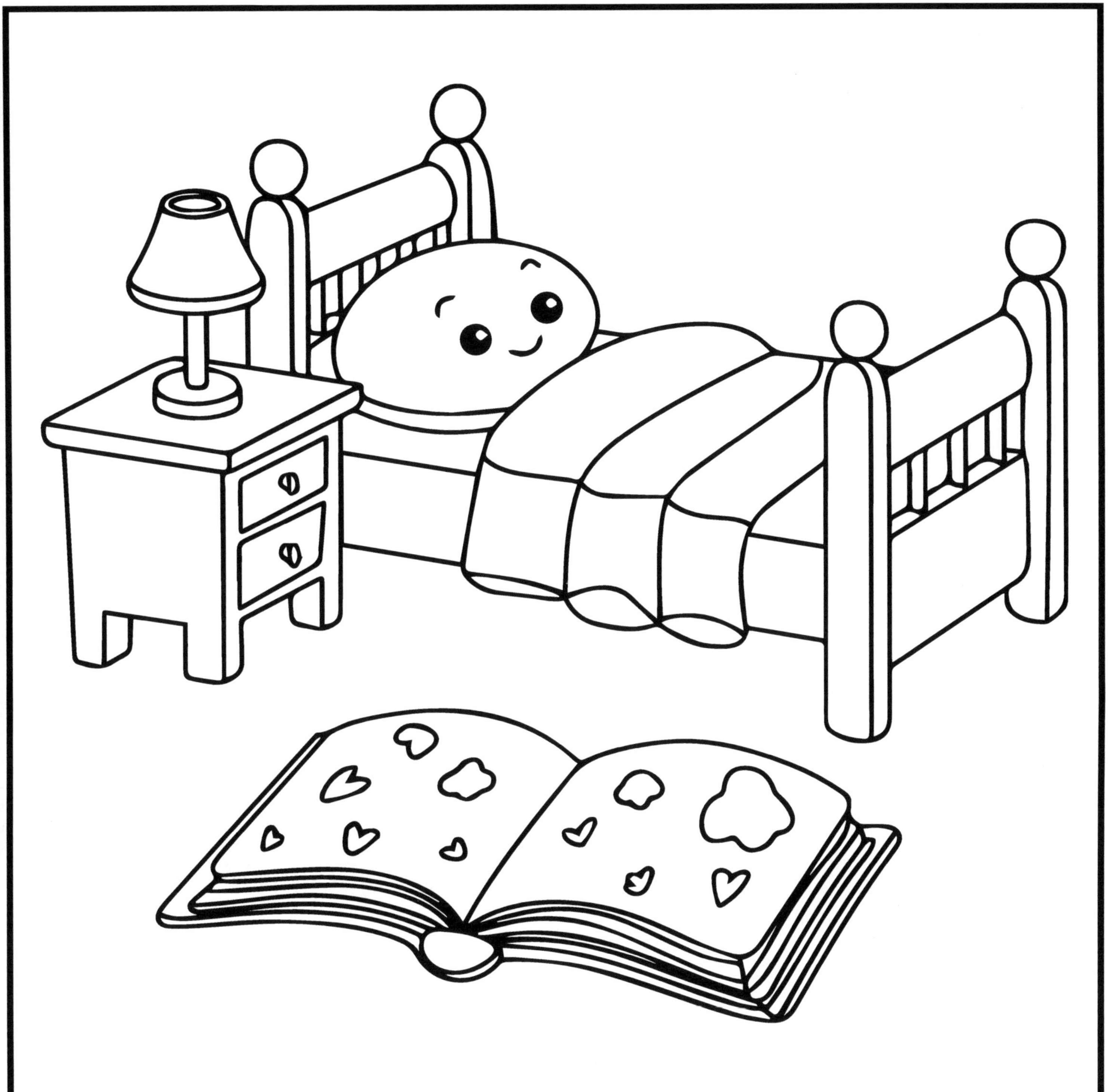

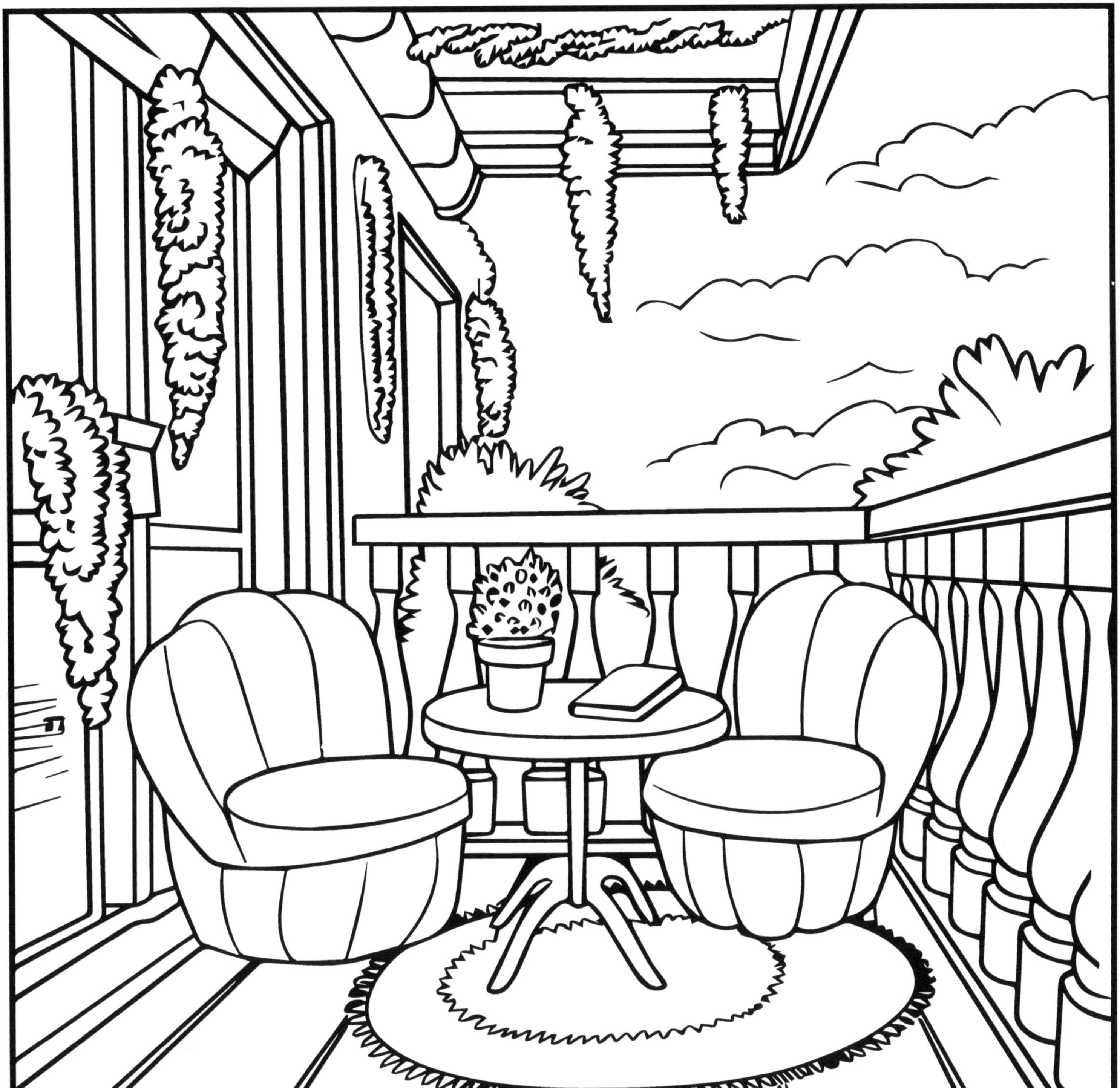

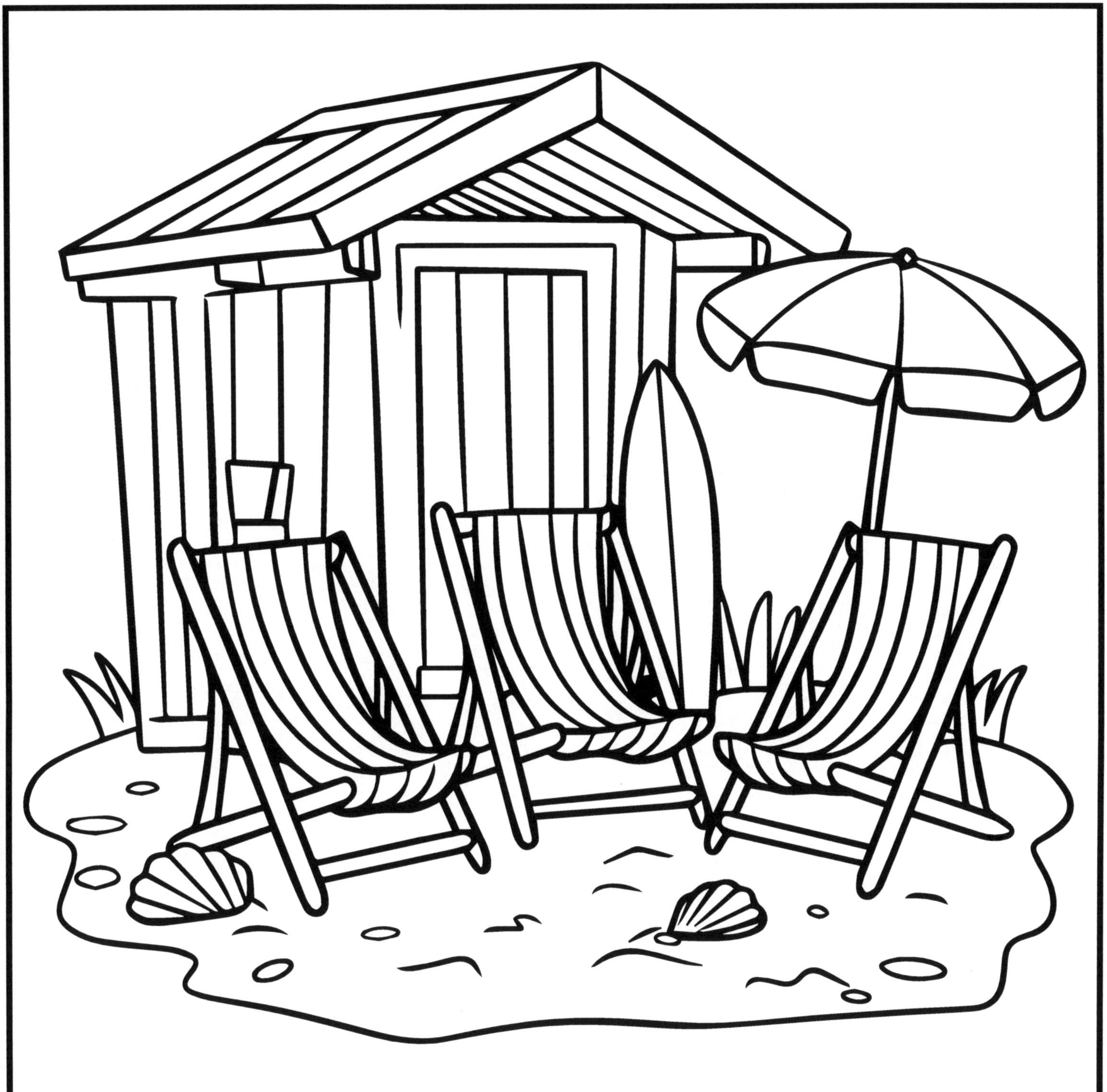

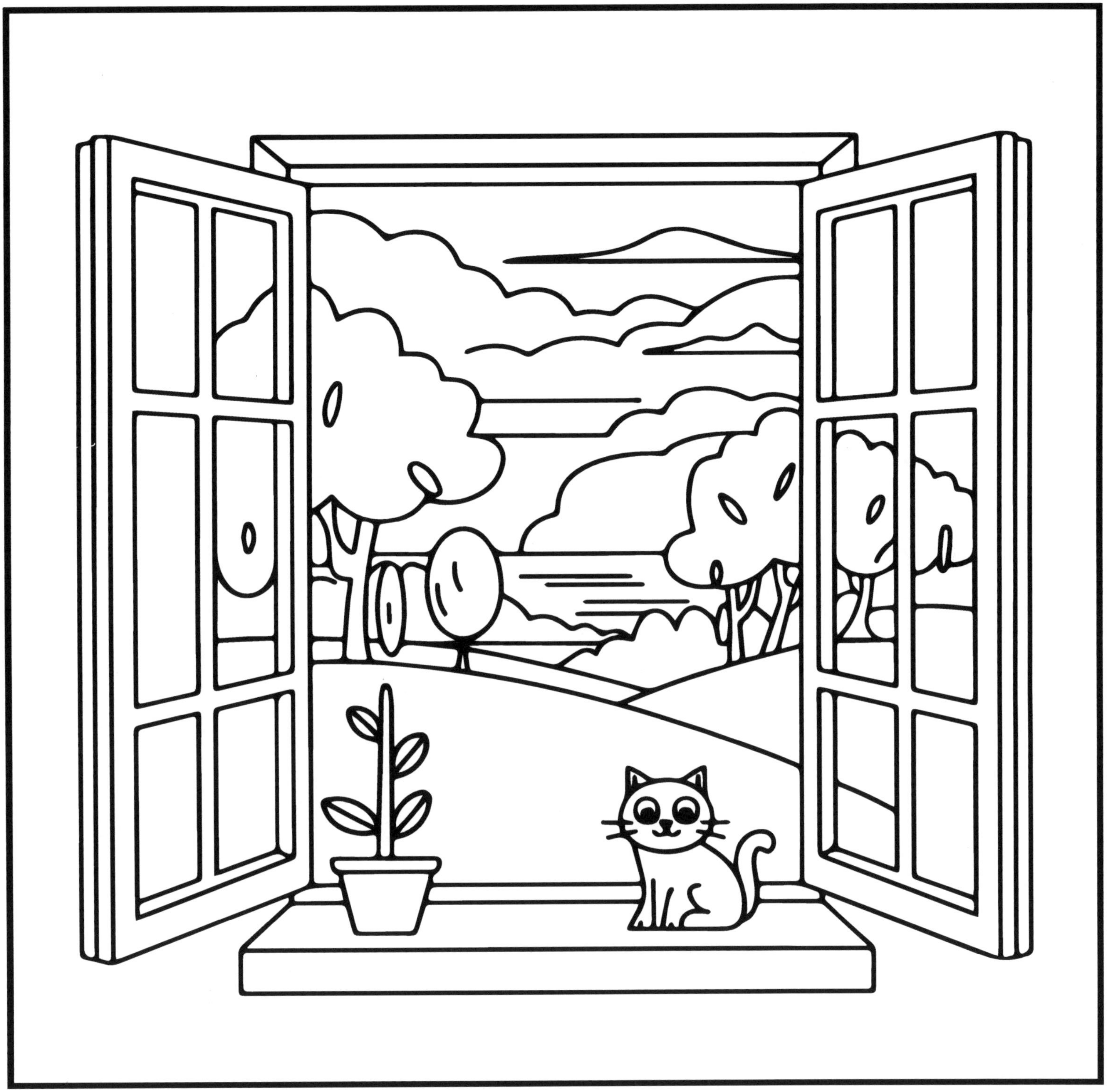

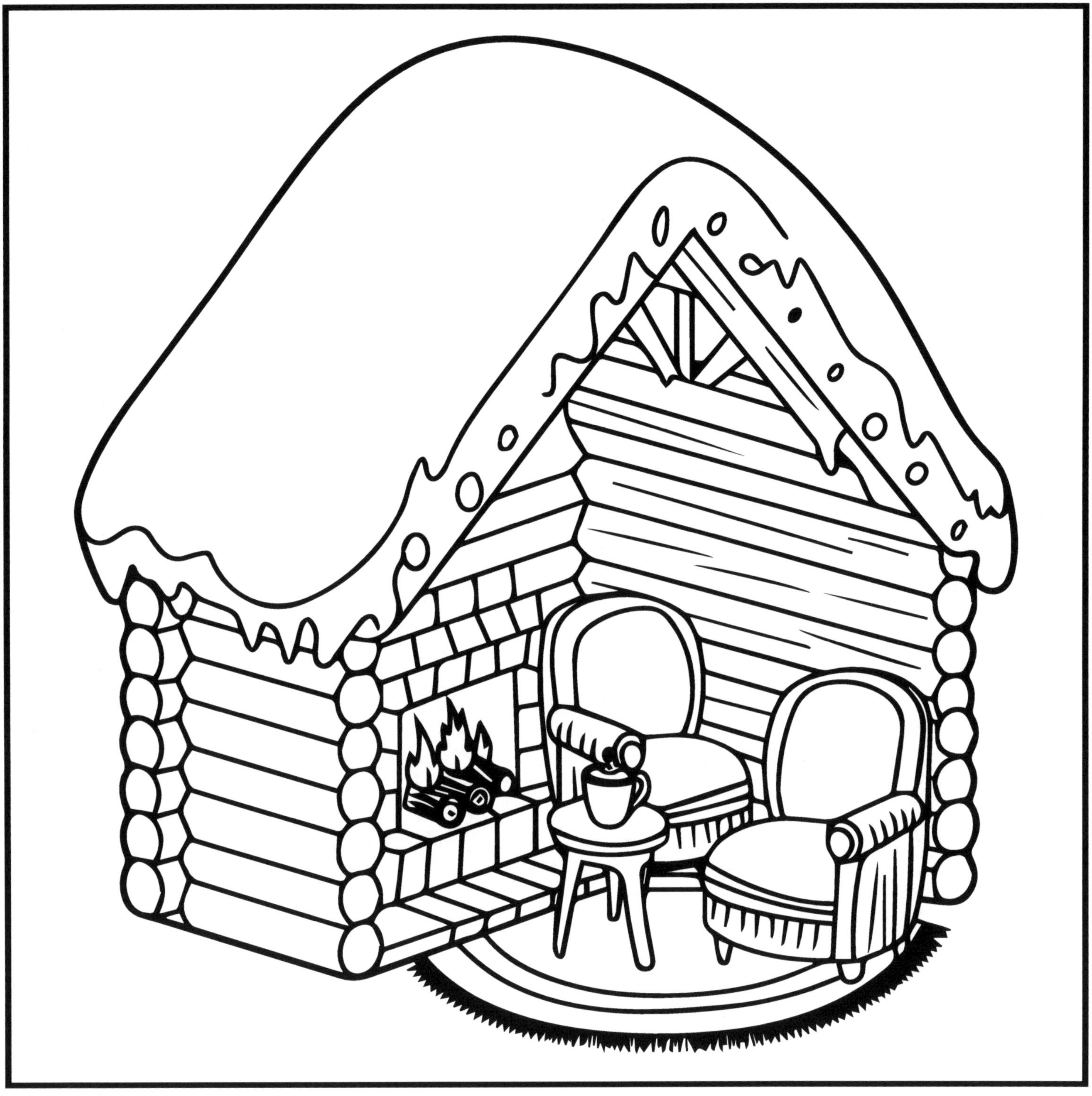

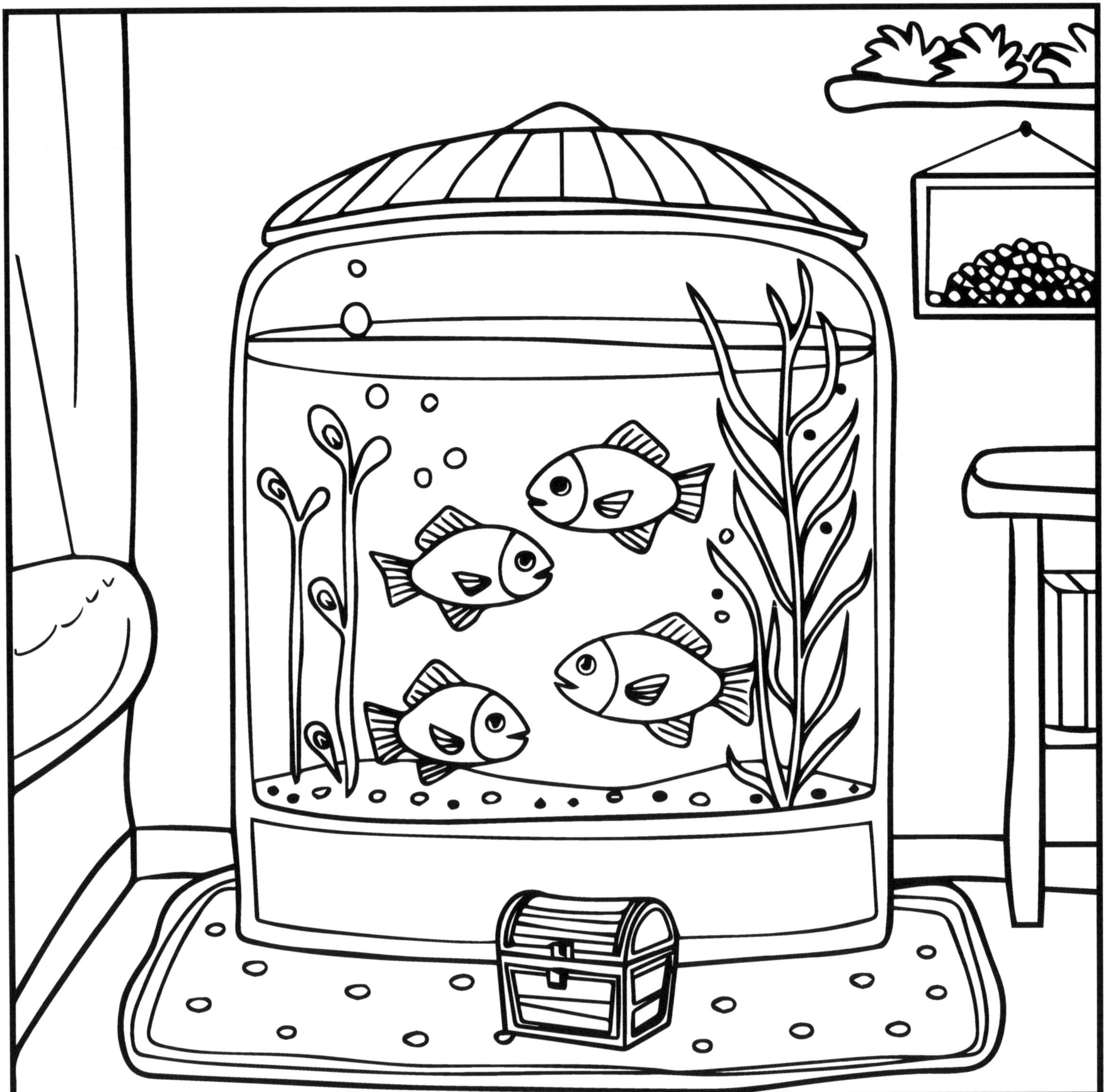

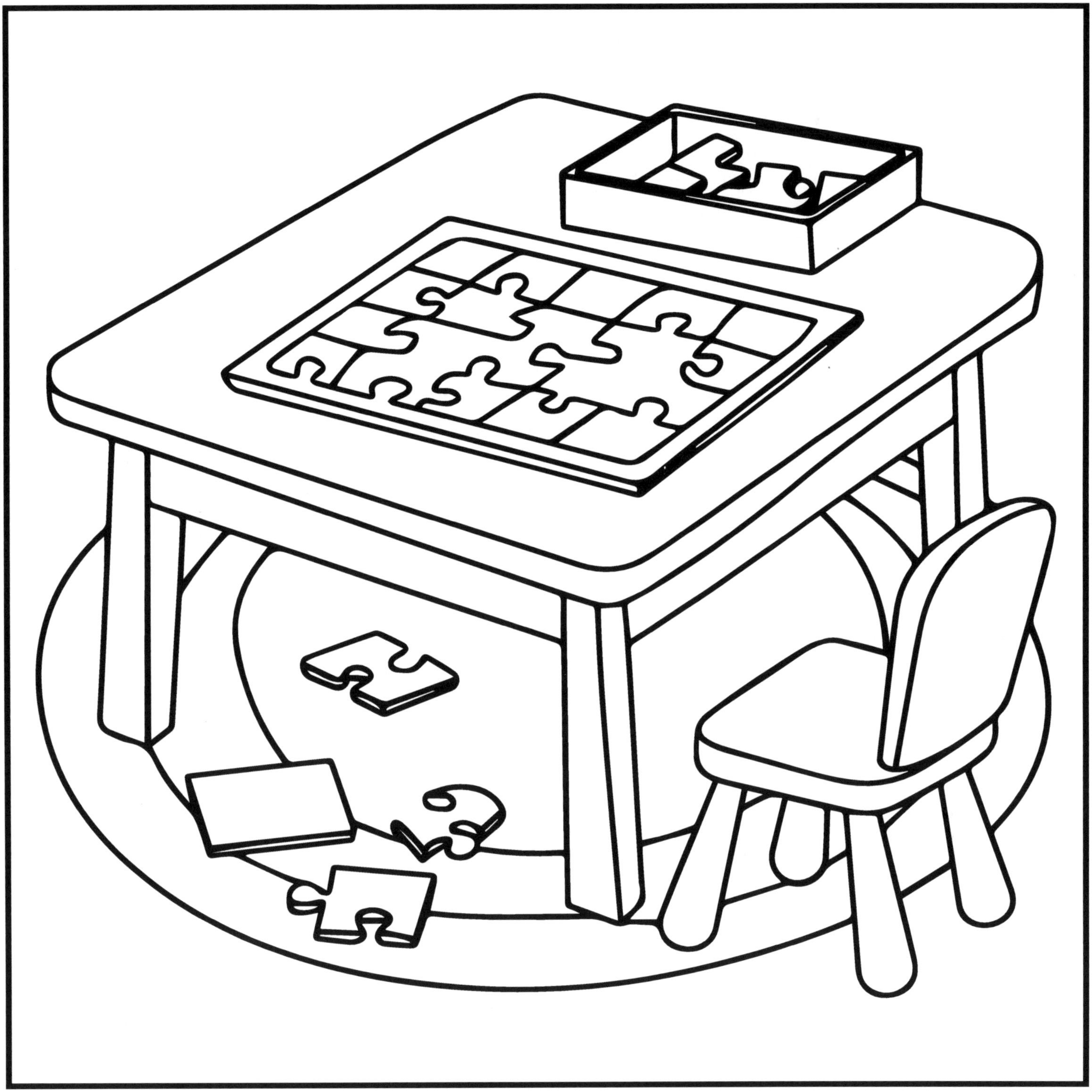

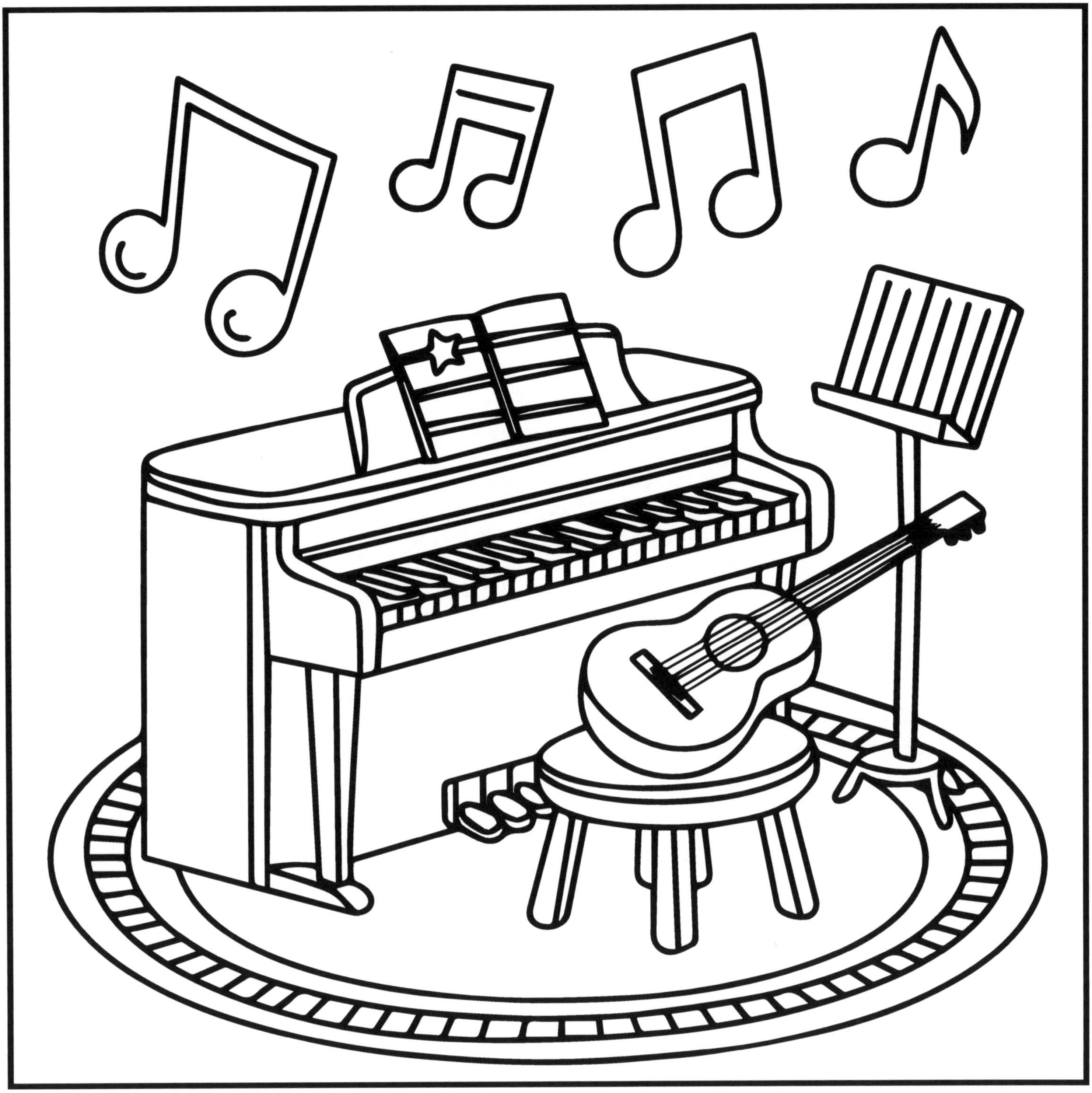

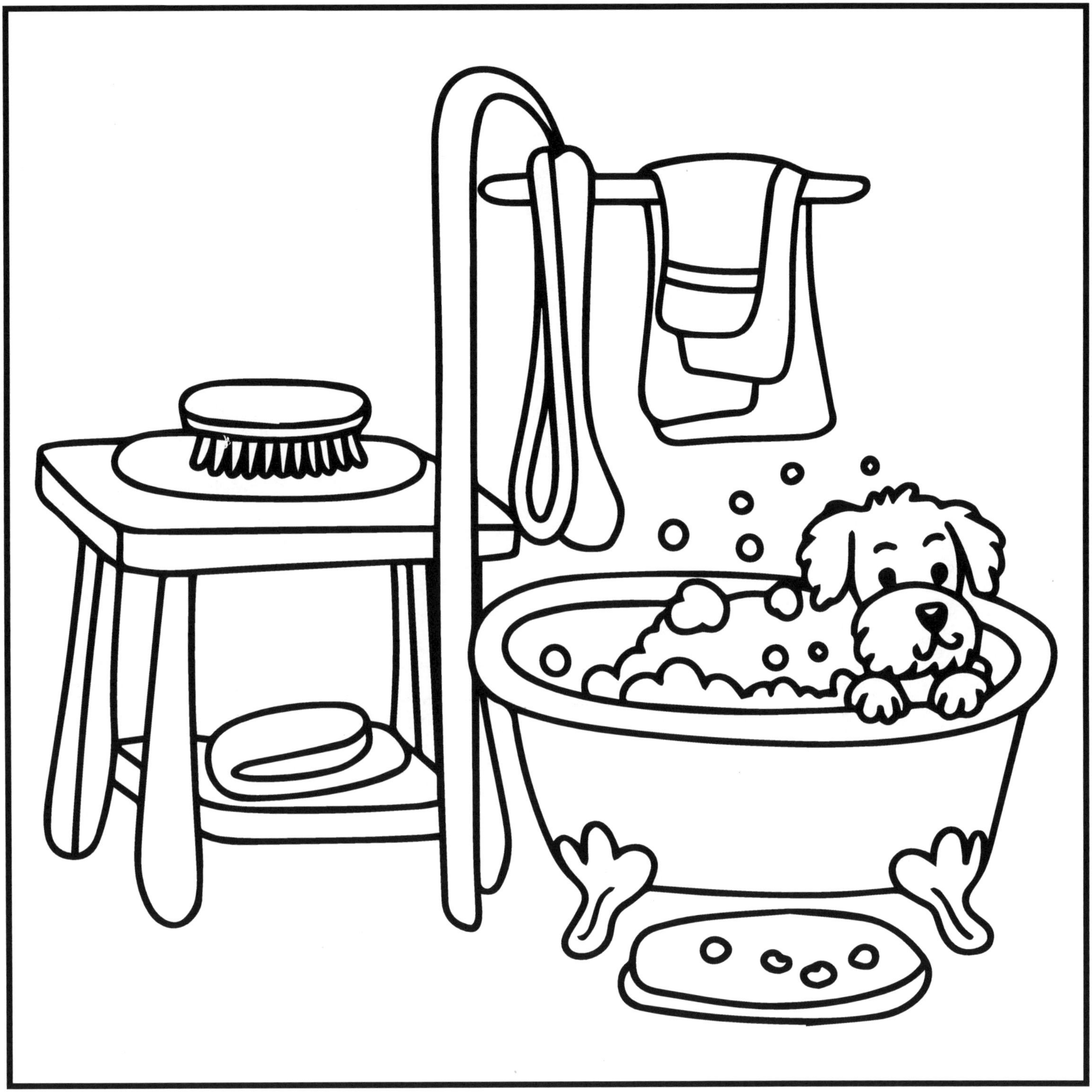

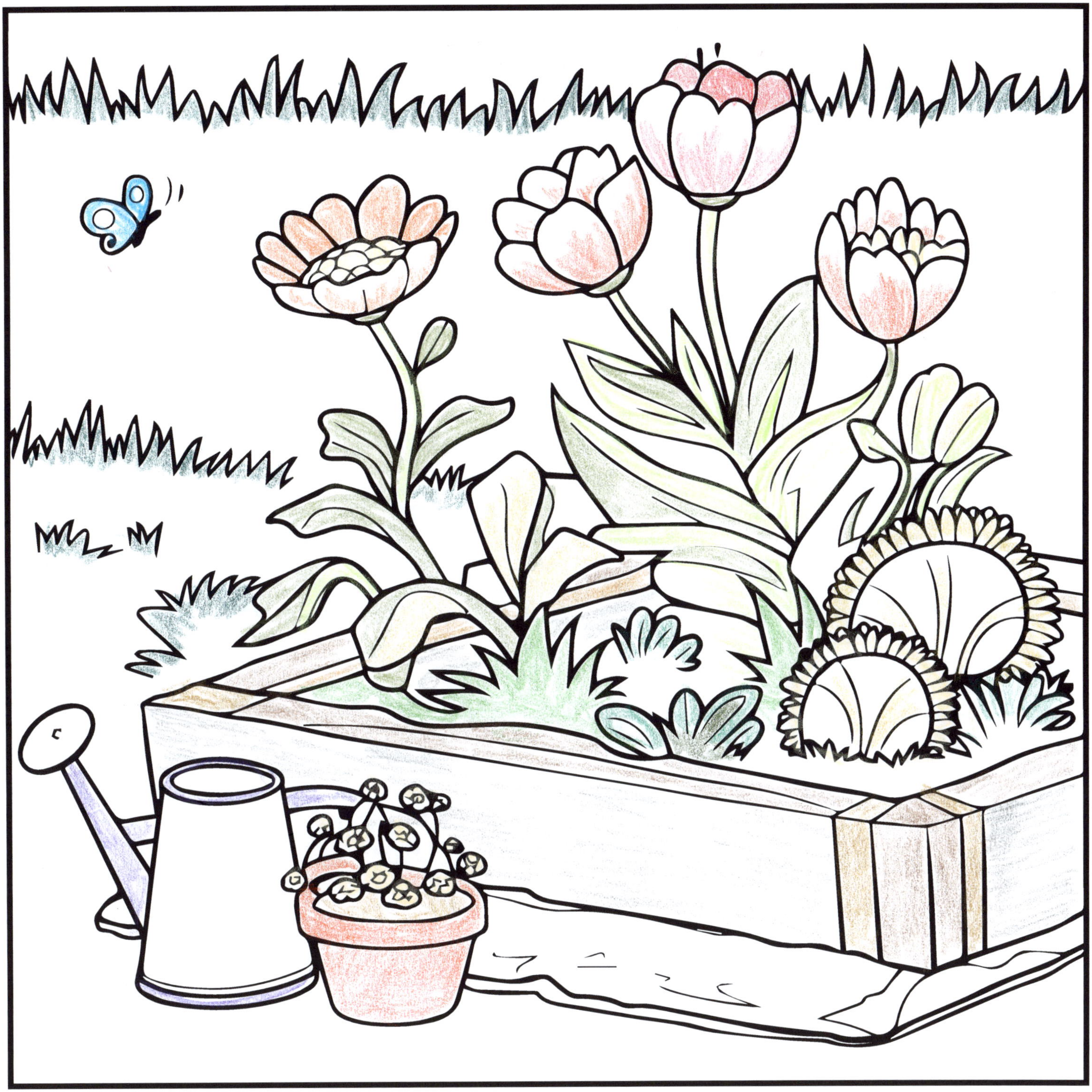

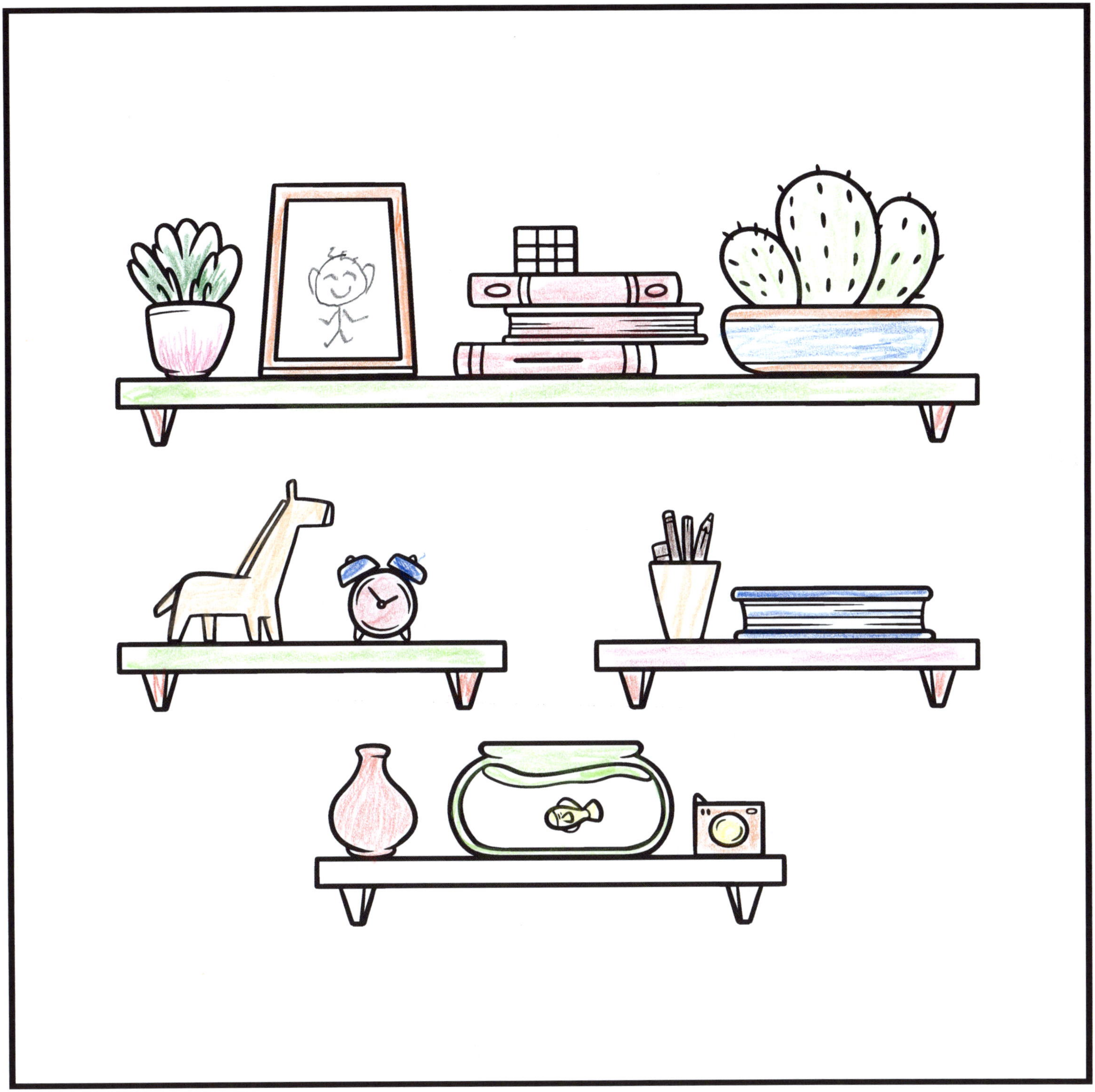

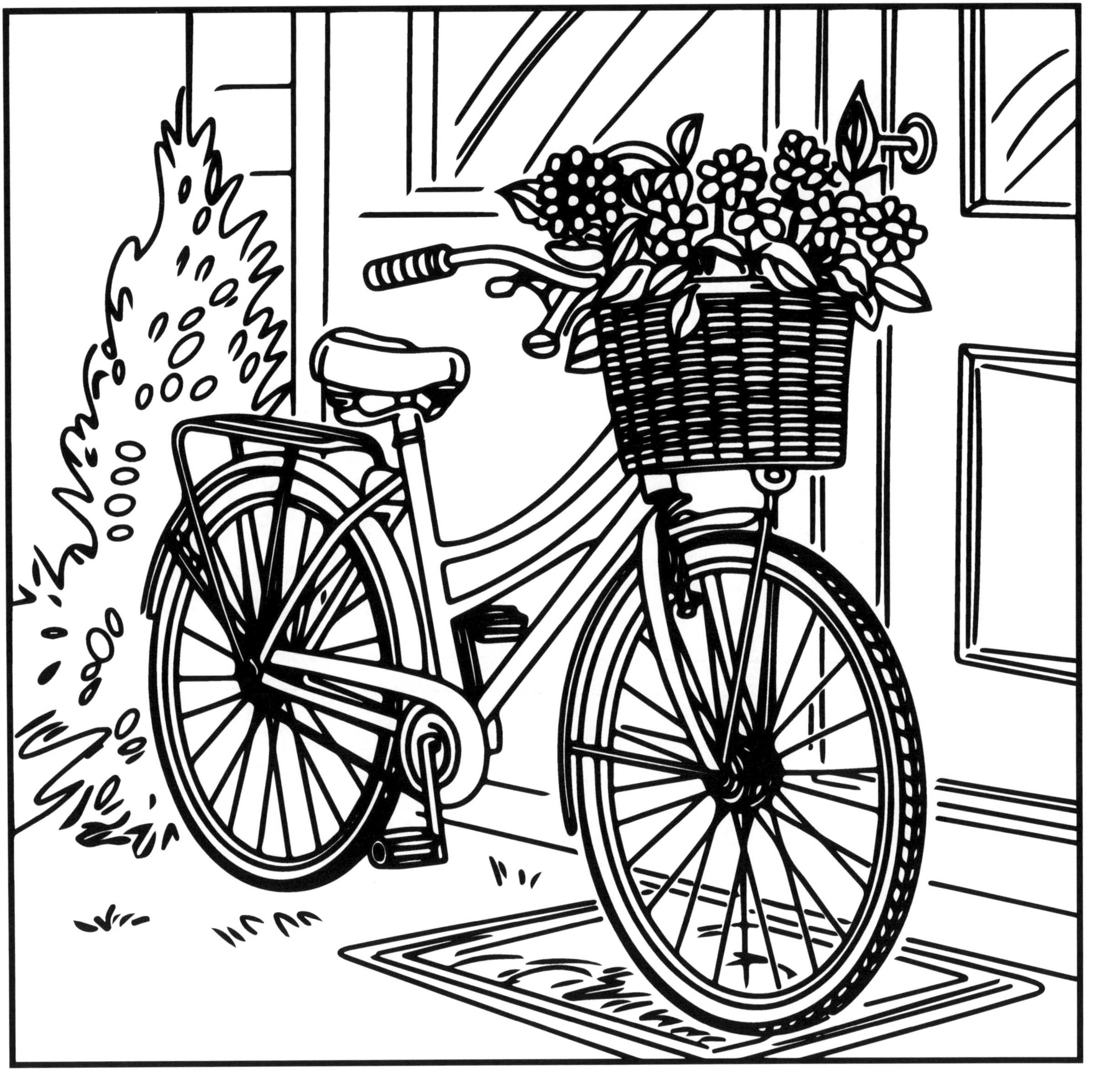

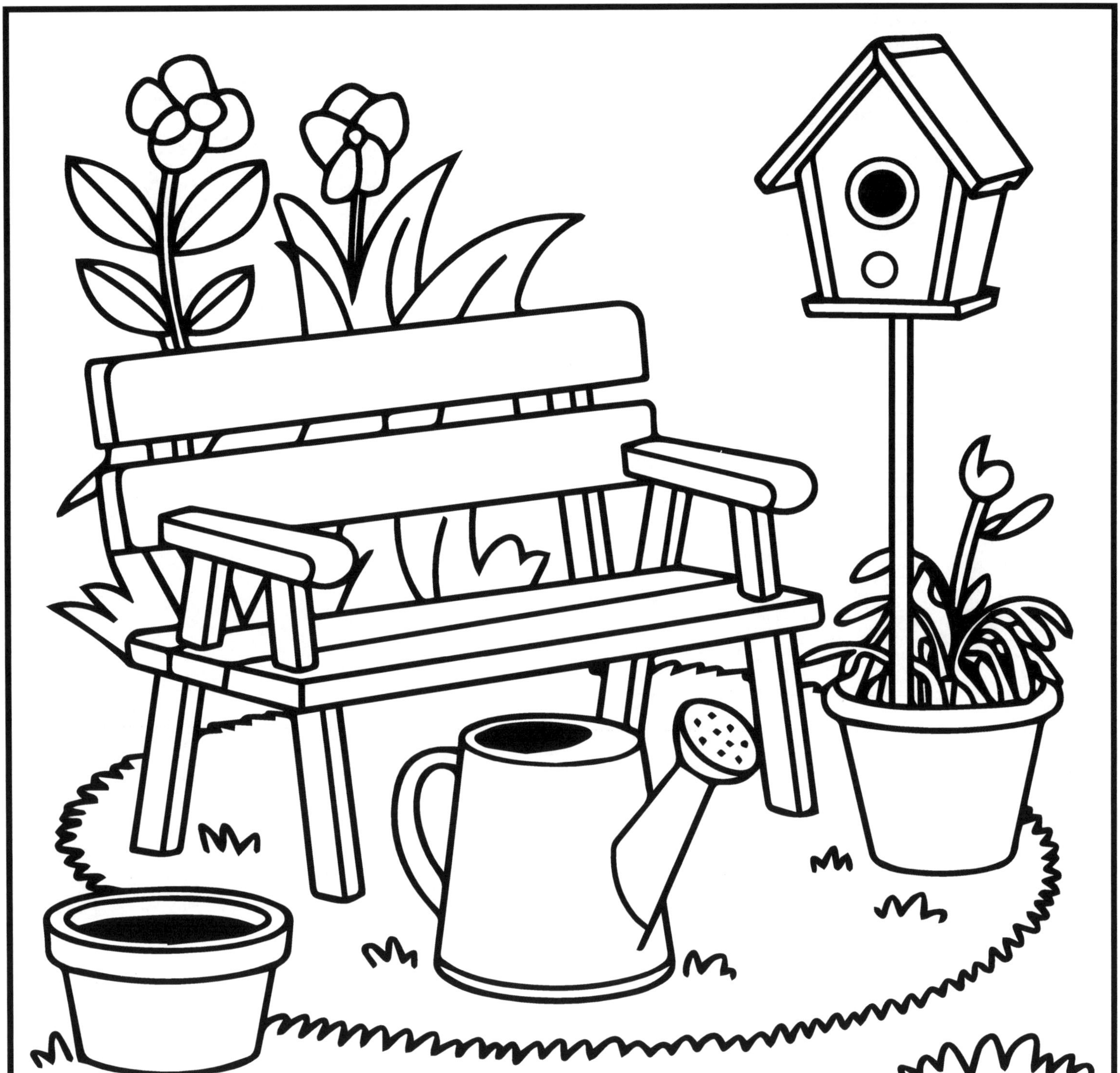

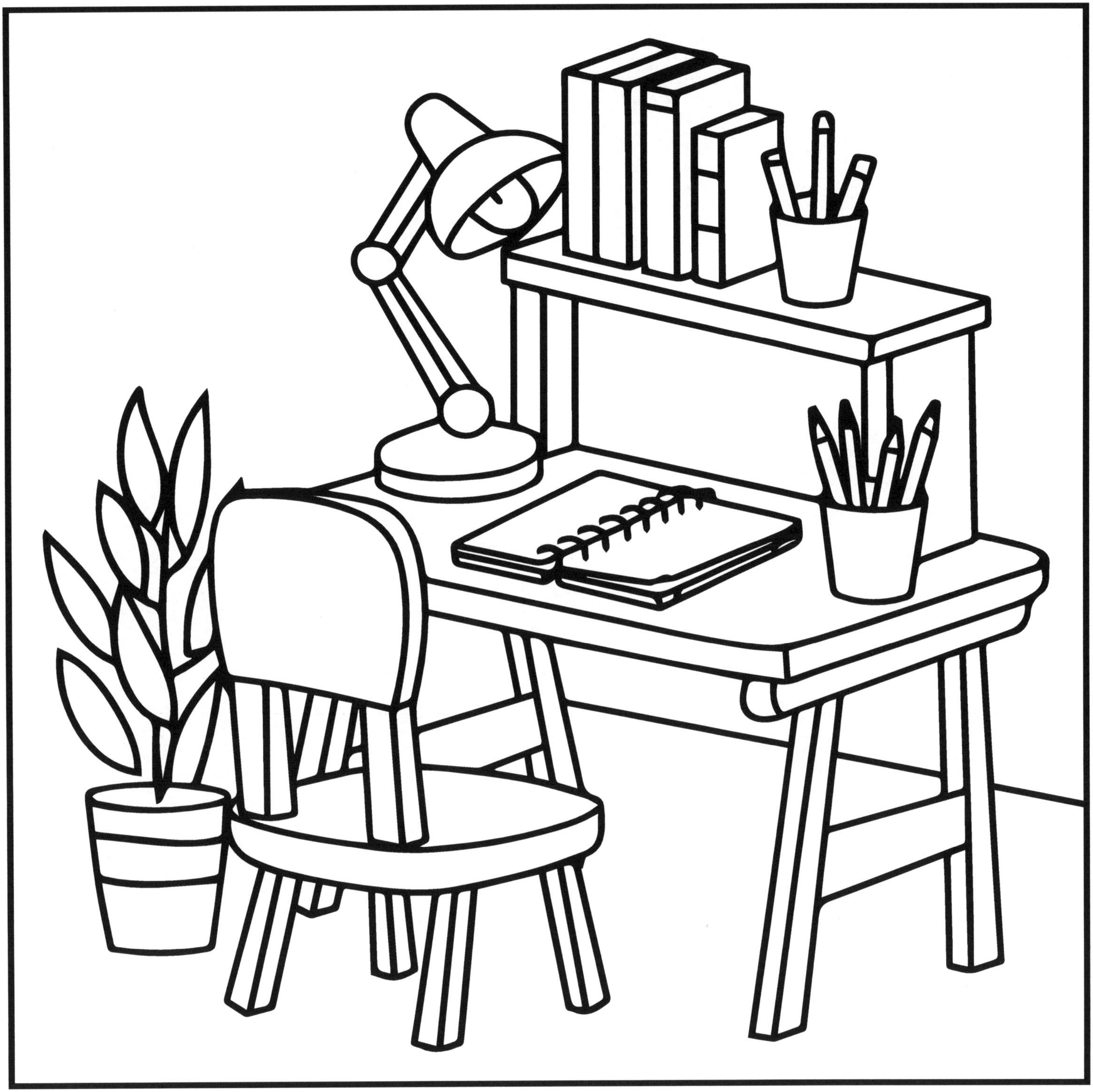

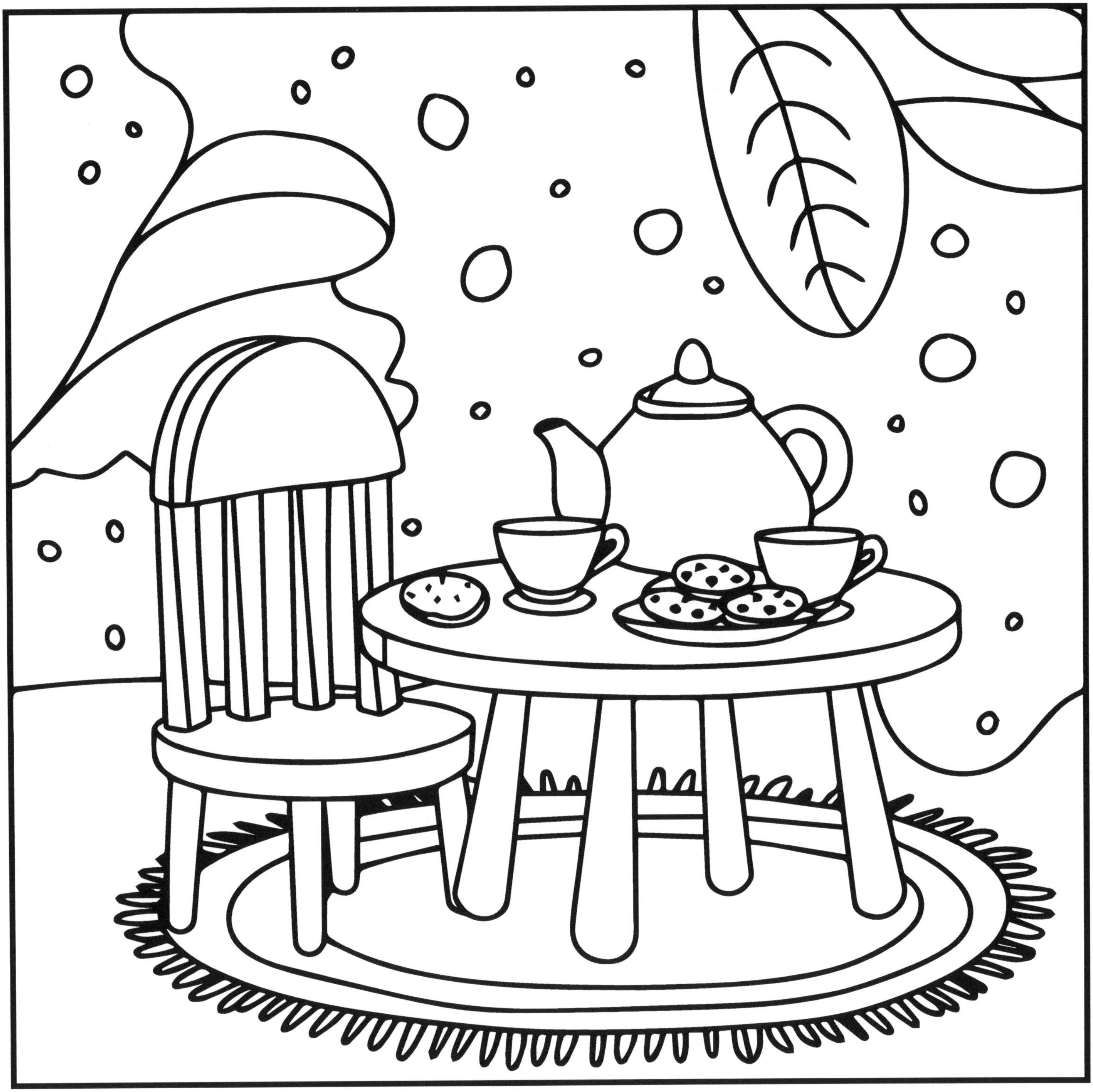

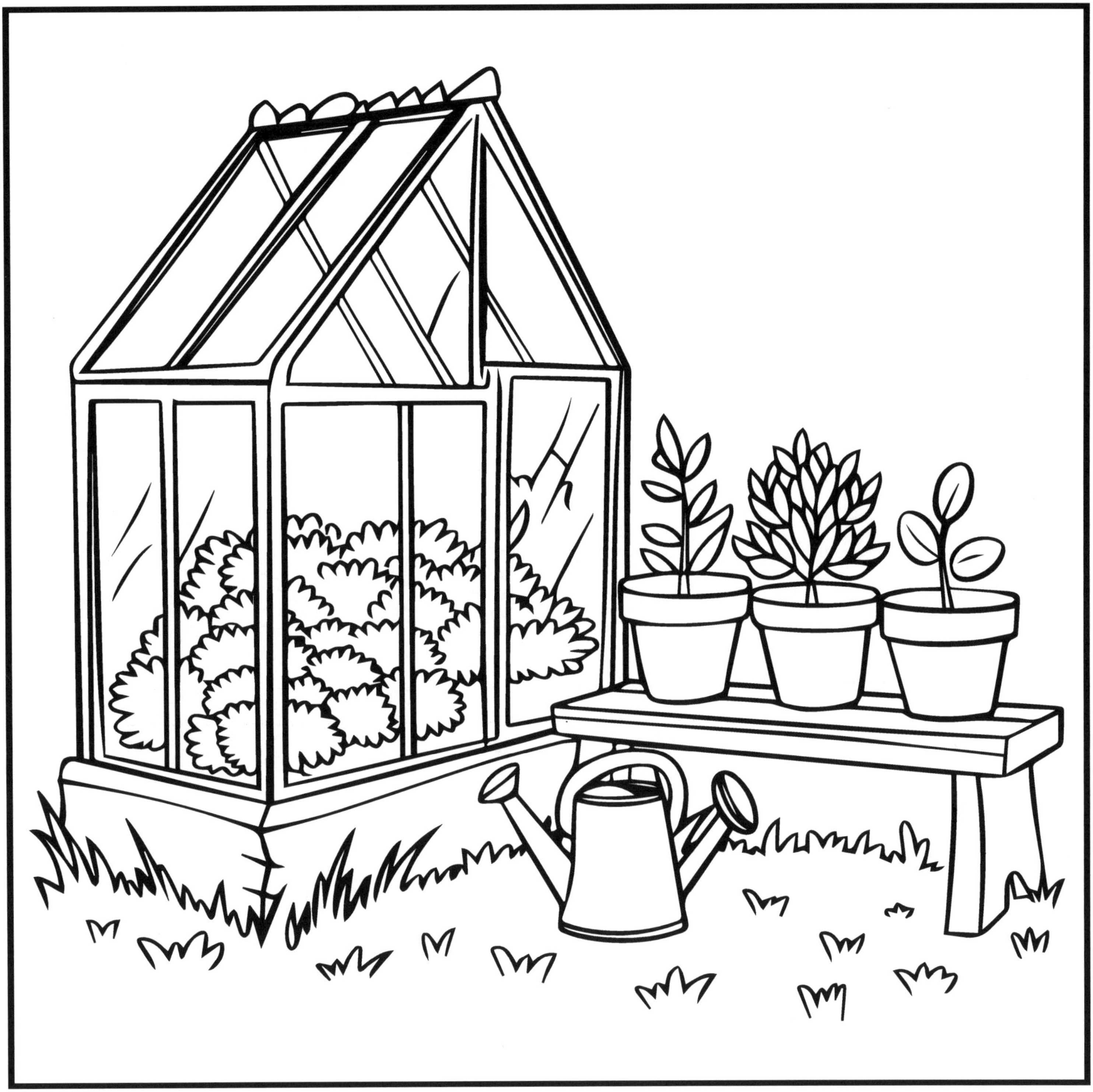

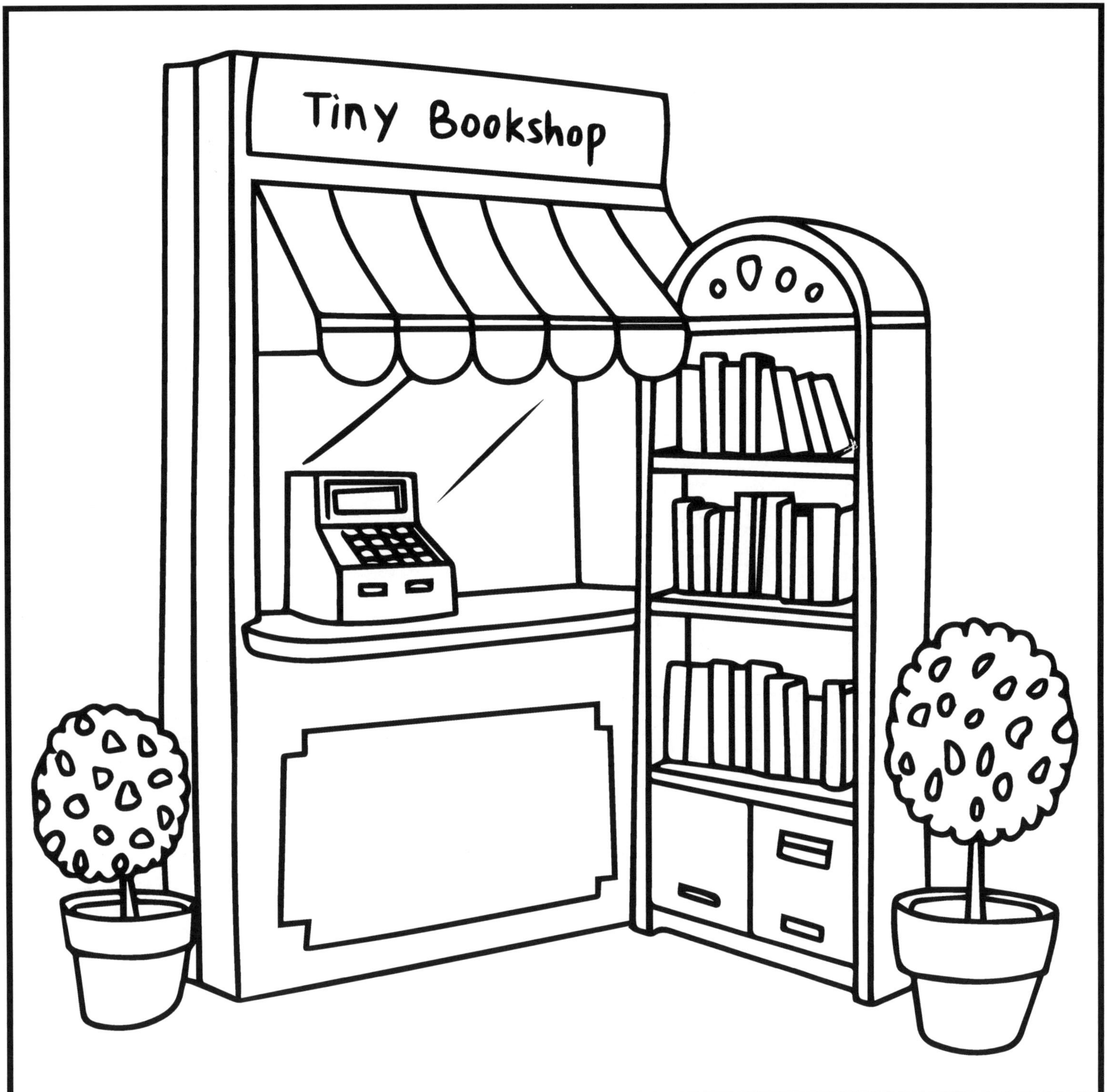
Tiny Bookshop

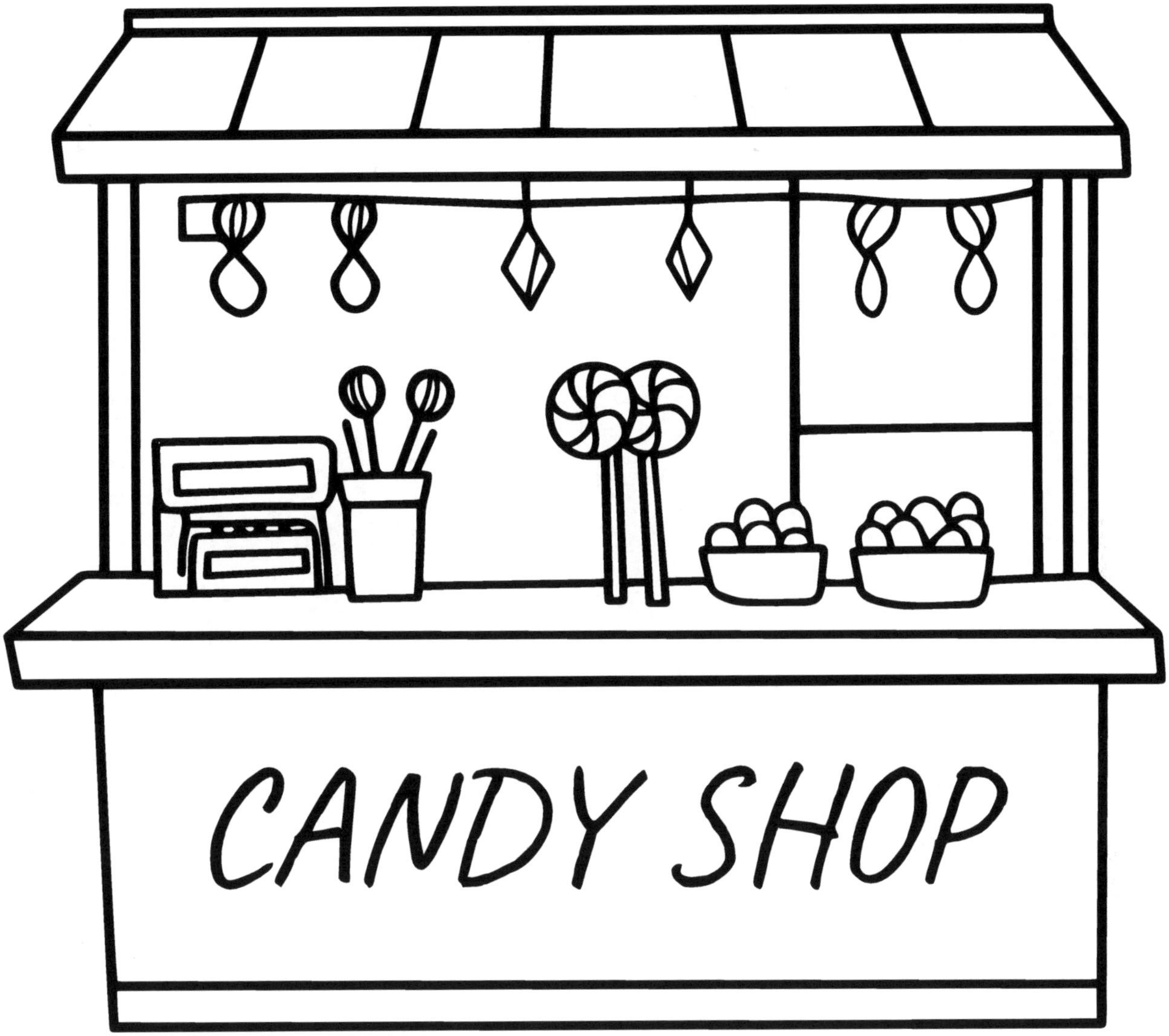
CANDY SHOP

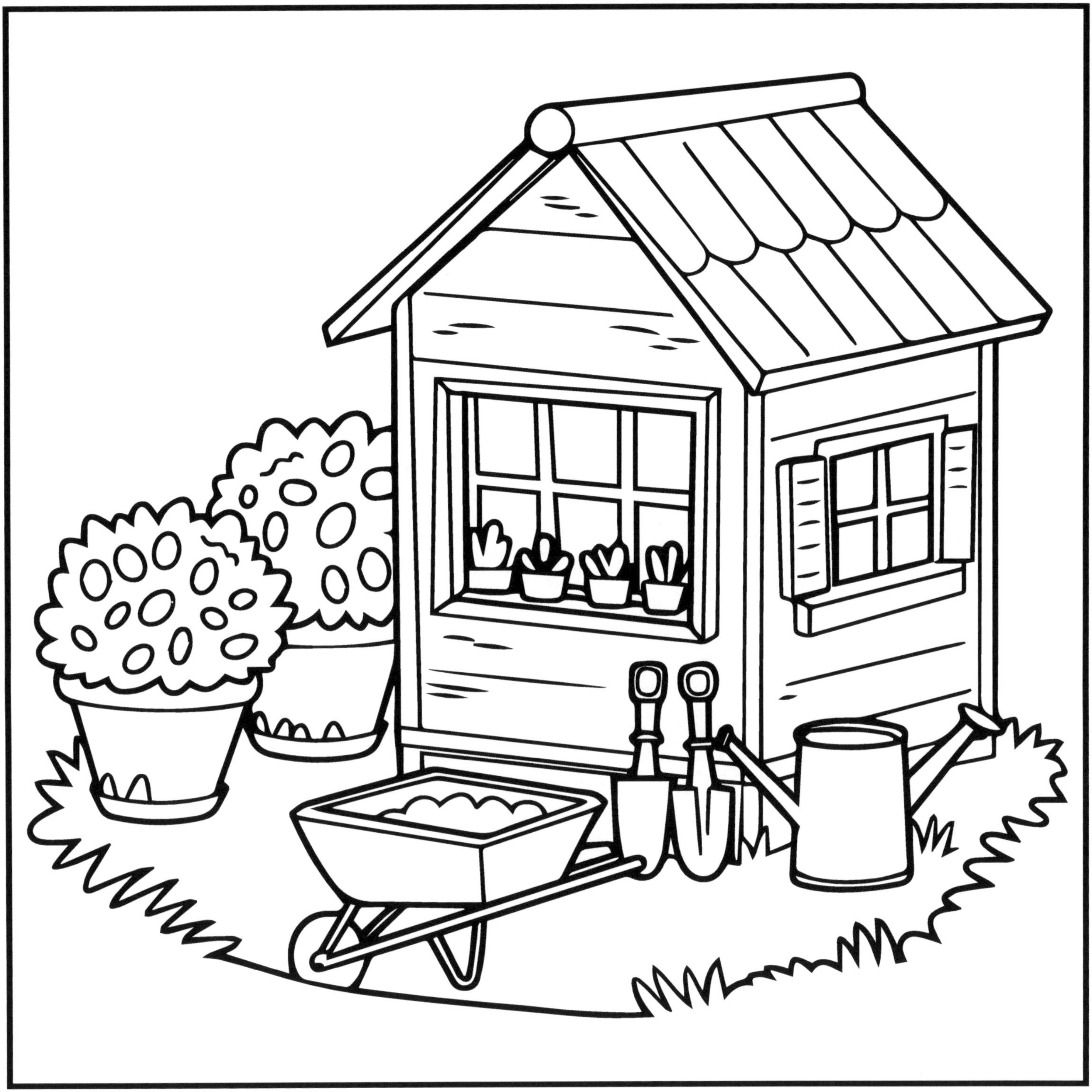

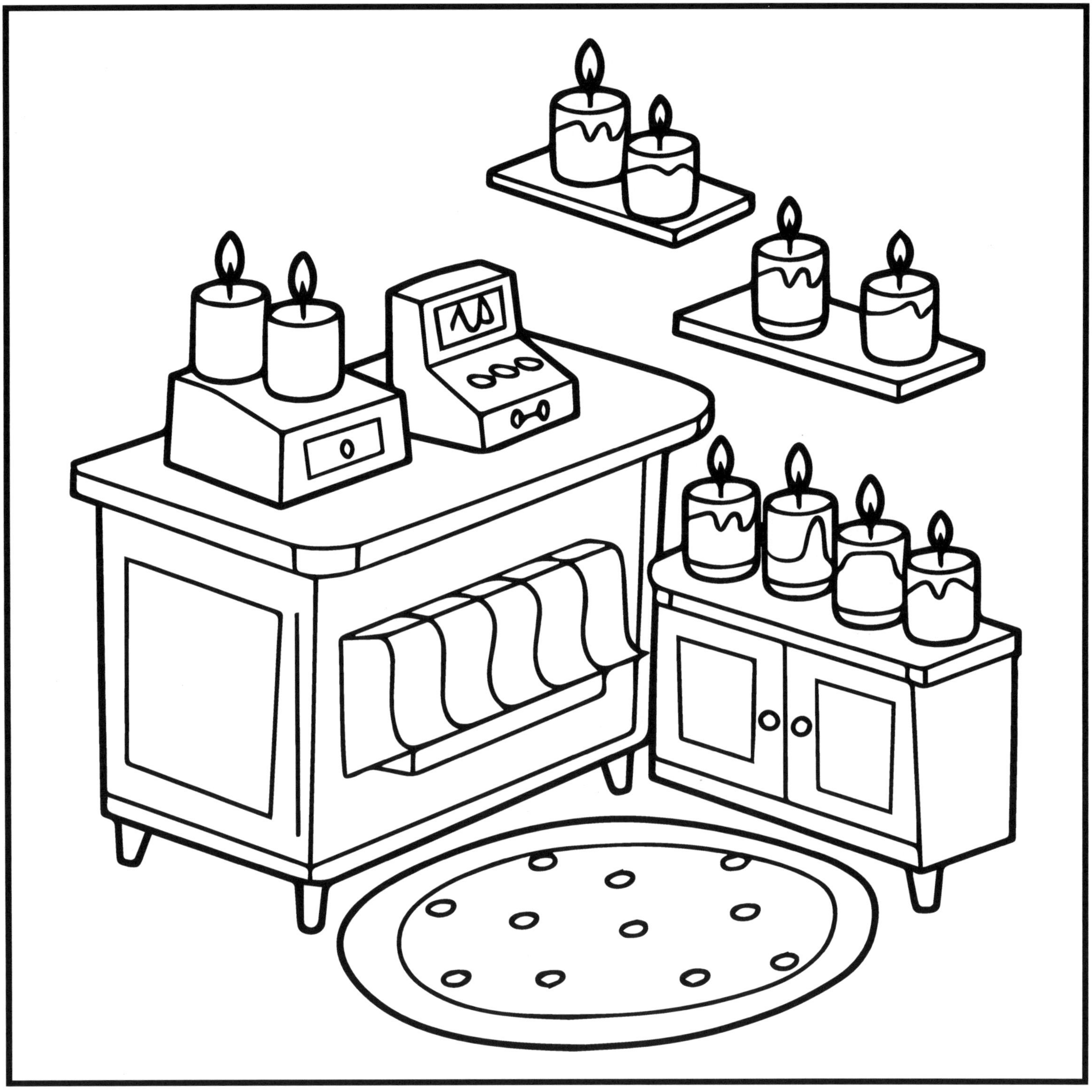

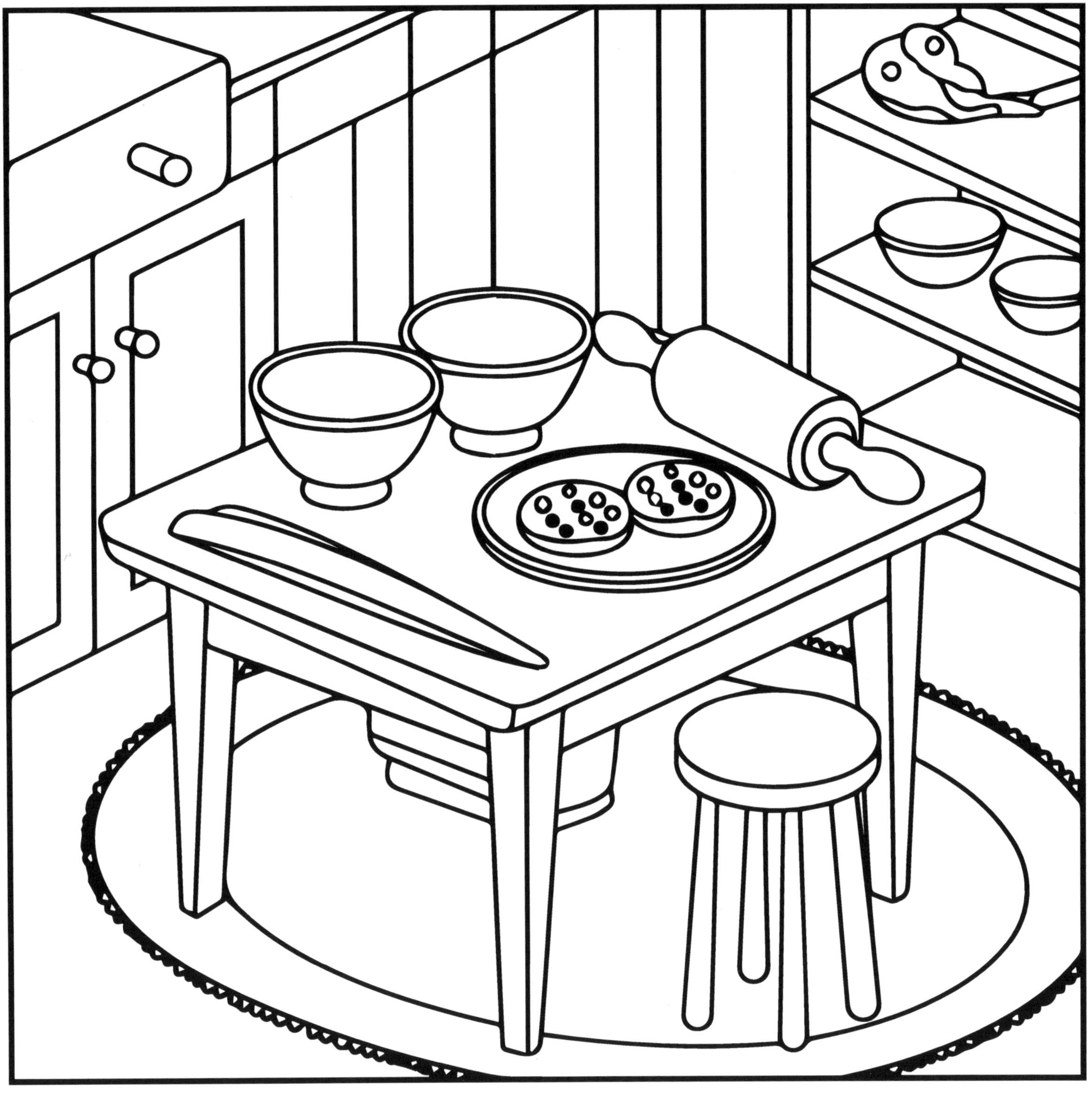

Thank you for choosing Milo Niro - enjoy your coloring !

Claim Your Free gift

Printed in Great Britain
by Amazon

53302392R00046